W L D

GRACE

WHAT HAPPENS WHEN GRACE HAPPENS

By MAX LUCADO

Adapted for teens by JAMES LUND

THOMAS NELSON
Since 1798

NASHVILLE   DALLAS   MEXICO CITY   RIO DE JANEIRO

[N O T E]

The text of *Wild Grace* was adapted from Max Lucado's book *Grace*. Gray boxes behind the text indicate places where new words and stories were added by James Lund specifically for our teen readers.

© 2012 by Max Lucado

Karen Hill, Executive Editor for Max Lucado.

Adapted for teens by James Lund.

Published in Nashville, Tennessee, by Tommy Nelson®. Tommy Nelson is a registered trademark of Thomas Nelson, Inc.

Tommy Nelson, Inc., titles may be purchased in bulk for educational, business, fund-raising, or sales promotional use. For information, please e-mail SpecialMarkets@ ThomasNelson.com.

Unless otherwise noted, Scripture quotations are taken from THE NEW KING JAMES VERSION. © 1982 by Thomas Nelson, Inc. Used by permission. All rights reserved.

Scripture quotations marked AMP are from THE AMPLIFIED BIBLE: NEW TESTAMENT. © 1958 by the Lockman Foundation (used by permission). CEB from the Common English Bible. © 2011 by Common English Bible. All rights reserved. MSG from *The Message* by Eugene H. Peterson. © 1993, 1994, 1995, 1996, 2000. Used by permission of NavPress Publishing Group. All rights reserved. NASB from NEW AMERICAN STANDARD BIBLE®. © The Lockman Foundation 1960, 1962, 1963, 1968, 1971, 1972, 1973, 1975, 1977. Used by permission. NCV from New Century Version®. © 2005 by Thomas Nelson, Inc. Used by permission. All rights reserved. NEB from THE NEW ENGLISH BIBLE. © 1961, 1970 by The Delegates of the Oxford University Press and the Syndics of the Cambridge University Press. Reprinted by permission. NIV from HOLY BIBLE: NEW INTERNATIONAL VERSION®. © 1973, 1978, 1984 by International Bible Society. Used by permission of Zondervan Publishing House. All rights reserved. NLT from *Holy Bible*, New Living Translation. © 1996. Used by permission of Tyndale House Publishers, Inc., Wheaton, Illinois 60189. All rights reserved. TLB from *The Living Bible*. © 1971. Used by permission of Tyndale House Publishers, Inc., Wheaton, Illinois 60189. All rights reserved.

Cover design by Studiogearbox.

Library of Congress Cataloging-in-Publication Data

Lucado, Max.
  Wild grace : what happens when grace happens / by Max Lucado ; adapted by James Lund.
    p. cm.
  ISBN 978-1-4003-2084-4 (pbk.)
  1. Christian teenagers—Religious life. 2. Christian teenagers—Conduct of life. 3. Grace (Theology) I. Lund, James L. II. Title.
  BV4531.3.L83125 2012
  248.8'3—dc23   2012018285

Printed in the United States of America

12 13 14 15 16 QG 6 5 4 3

For Daniel and Andrew Ligon. I have watched the two of you grow into billboards of grace. You inspire me! May God continue to fill and use you.

CONTENTS

ACKNOWLEDGMENTS

I'm waving a banner of gratitude to these folks who made *Wild Grace* possible:

James Lund—Your ability to relate to teens is exceptional. Thanks for your great work.

Michelle Prater Burke—Thanks for shepherding this book from idea to completion.

Laura Minchew and the rest of the Thomas Nelson team—You're more than colleagues; you're friends. I'm grateful.

Shelby Di Giosia and Nathan Crosby, our teen editors—Your insights were super. Thanks!

PART 1

GOD, GRACE, AND YOU

THE GRACE
ADVENTURE

God's grace has a drenching about it. A
wildness about it. A whitewater, riptide,
turn-you-upside-downness about it. Grace
comes after you.

You steer your kayak downriver, your heart hammering like a hummingbird's wings against your chest. Are you ready for this? No turning back now. The swirling eddies and cascading currents that lead to Monster Rock are just ahead.

You surge forward, the foam flying and rapids roaring. A shout escapes your lips before you even realize it: "Wooooohooooo!"

This is living.

Quick paddle strokes move you past one boulder, then another. Suddenly, there it is. A black mound bigger than your garage. The Mother of All River Rocks.

You know from scouting this spot that the current is your true enemy. You've got to veer left, before the raging water takes your cork of a craft, slams it against stone, and mashes you into pumpkin pulp. Time to paddle!

An overworked waitress approaches a regular customer and asks, "Do you know the difference between you and a kayak?" The customer shakes his head no. "Sometimes," the waitress says, "a kayak tips."

You pull with all your strength. Your heart is beating so loudly that you're scared your eardrums will explode.

Left! Left! Are you going to make it?

Suddenly, you shoot through the mist into calmer waters. You did it! You've conquered the Monster!

Only a moment ago your heart was pounding like a drummer on steroids. Relentless. Desperate. Now the danger has passed. You've pushed through the moment of near panic. And your heart is changing. From rushing like a freight train to the calm *thump . . . thump . . . thump . . .* of a heart at rest.

If only it were that easy to change the *rest* of your heart. You know, the part that houses those other monsters. I'm talking about selfishness. Superiority. Anger. Greed. Guilt.

Nope, no easy switch for any of us. But for God? Not a problem. He's in the business of changing hearts.

We would be wrong to think this change happens overnight. But we would be equally wrong to assume change never happens at all. It may come in fits and spurts, an "aha" here, a breakthrough there. But it comes.

Could you use some?

You stare into the darkness. Your cat slumbers at the foot of your bed. The ceiling fan whirls above you. In fifteen minutes the alarm will sound and zoom you like a snowboarder on a half-pipe into another free-for-all with teachers, classmates, teammates, and friends-who-might-not-be-friends. For the millionth time, you'll make your bed, breakfast, the bus, and homework deadlines . . . but for the life of you, you can't make sense of this thing called life. Its beginnings and endings. Makeups and breakups and due dates and drama and questions. What's it all about anyway?

You turn the page of your Bible and stare at the words. You might as well be gazing at a graveyard. Lifeless and stony. Nothing moves you. You yawn through the daily reading with the same barely awake expression you save for sixth-period calculus. But you don't dare close the book, no sirree. You're afraid God will give up on you if you do.

You run your finger over the photo of your mom's face. You promised her you'd never touch drugs. Then your best friend asked if you wanted to smoke some pot. You were curious. You only meant to try it once. But once became twice became a few times a week. Now it's practically a habit. Even worse, your mom guessed something was up. When she asked if you or your friends had ever tried marijuana, you said

no. You lied to her face! Now you feel terrible. How are
you supposed to fix this?

You listen to the preacher. A tubby sort with jowls,
a bald dome, and a thick neck that hangs over
his clerical collar. Your dad makes you come to
church, but he can't make you listen. At least, that
is what you've always muttered to yourself. But this
morning you listen because the minister speaks of a
God who loves prodigals, and you feel like the worst
sort of one. You can't keep the pregnancy a secret
much longer. Soon your parents will know. The
preacher will know. He says God knows already. You
wonder what God thinks.

YOUR STORY:

What's the biggest problem you're dealing with right now?

....

Do you have a plan to solve it?

....

On a scale of 1 to 10, 1 being "no sweat" and 10 being "I'm
doomed," how confident are you in your plan?

....

Where does God fit into this picture?

....

It doesn't get easier, does it? Bad hair days. Bad class days. Bad choices that ruin families, friendships, and futures, making you feel like a failure. Will you ever figure it all out?

God answers the junk of life with one word: *grace*.

We talk like we understand the term. The library gives us a *grace* period to pay a late fine. The no-good politician falls from *grace*. Musicians speak of a *grace* note. We describe an actress as *gracious*, a dancer as *graceful*. We use the word for hospitals, baby girls, kings, and premeal prayers. We talk like we know what *grace* means.

> Could there be more to grace than bowed heads at dinner and "Good bread, good meat, good God, let's eat"?

Especially at church. *Grace* graces the songs we sing and the Bible verses we read. *Grace* shares the church office with its cousins: *forgiveness*, *faith*, and *fellowship*. Preachers explain it. Hymns proclaim it. Bible schools teach it.

> One dictionary definition of "grace" is "unmerited divine assistance." Sounds simple enough— God giving us something we don't deserve. But do we really *get* grace? And even if we do, does it have anything to do with our lives?

Here's my hunch: we've settled for wimpy grace. It politely occupies a phrase in a hymn, fits nicely on a church sign. Never causes trouble or demands a response. When asked, "Do you believe in grace?" who could say no?

This book asks deeper questions: Have you been changed by grace? Shaped by grace? Strengthened by grace? Emboldened by grace? Softened by grace? Snatched by the nape of your neck and shaken to your senses by grace? God's grace has a drenching about it. A wildness about it. A whitewater, riptide, turn-you-upside-downness about it. Grace comes after you. It rewires you. From insecure to God-secure. From regret-riddled to better-because-of-it. From afraid to die to ready to fly. Grace is the voice that calls us to change and then gives us the power to pull it off.[1] Once you encounter it, you'll never be the same.

> Have you been changed by grace?

A girl named Shannon understands. As she drove to high school on the third day of her junior year, her biggest worries were memorizing her class schedule, locker combination, and pep-squad routines.

Oh, and one more thing: lipstick. She'd forgotten to put it on that morning.

Shannon was driving on a country road, the kind that features endless views of cornrows and clustered cows, but rarely people. Almost never, in fact. So Shannon adjusted her rearview mirror for a quick swipe on the lips. It took only a moment. When her eyes returned to the road, she glimpsed something moving directly in front of her.

The car jolted. Shannon braked. She'd hit something.

The sinking feeling in Shannon's gut turned to horror when she got out and saw the body of a woman lying facedown in the grass next to a mangled bicycle. Paramedics soon confirmed the worst. The woman, Marjorie Jarstfer, was dead.

Shannon wanted to join her. One thought kept running through her disbelieving brain: *I should have been the one killed, not her.*

Later, Shannon learned that the dead woman's husband, Gary, wanted her to meet him at his home the night before the funeral. That was the last thing Shannon wanted. She was terrified. Yet she knew she couldn't say no.

When Shannon stepped into the house that day, her heart raced. From the end of the entry corridor, a burly, middle-aged man approached. He opened his arms wide. Shannon couldn't believe it. He wasn't angry. He wanted a hug. This grieving husband embraced Shannon, and the tears she'd been holding back flowed freely onto his flannel shirt. "I'm so sorry," she said. "I'm so sorry."

Gary sat Shannon down and began to tell her about his wife. Marjorie loved and was close to the Lord. She'd told Gary she sensed she'd be going home soon. "You can't let this ruin your life, Shannon," Gary said. "God wants to strengthen you through this. He wants to use you. As a matter of fact, I am passing Marjorie's legacy of being a godly woman on to you. I want you to love Jesus without limits, just like Marjorie did."

Gary refused to press charges against Shannon or sue her family for damages beyond insurance. Shannon kept waiting for Gary to come to his

> Shannon couldn't believe it. He wasn't angry. He wanted a hug.

senses and dish out an appropriate punishment. It never happened.

Grace had chased Shannon from the moment she got in her car that fateful school-day morning. She finally let it catch her and, like Gary Jarstfer, wrap her in a bear hug that wouldn't let go. Shannon went from feeling guilty to feeling chosen. Her future was assured. She would live out Marjorie's legacy, a godly woman who loves Jesus beyond measure. Today, Shannon Ethridge is a best-selling Christian author, speaker, and counselor.[2]

What a difference grace made for Shannon. What a difference it can make for you. Can't forgive the friend who humiliated you in the cafeteria? Can't face your parents because you failed a test? Can't forgive yourself for the terrible thing you said or did yesterday? Christ can, and he is on the move, aggressively budging you from graceless to grace-shaped living. The gift-given giving gifts. Forgiven people forgiving people. Mistakes still? Of course. Despair? Rare.

> Grace is a certain beginning of glory in us.
>
> —Saint Thomas Aquinas

Grace is everything Jesus. Grace lives because he does, works because he works, and matters because he matters. To be saved by grace is to be saved by him, not by an idea, rule, or church membership, but by Jesus himself, who will sweep into heaven anyone who so much as gives him the nod.

Not, mind you, in response to a finger snap, a religious chant, or a secret handshake. Grace won't be stage-managed. It's like Jesus himself: uncontainable, untamable. Like a wild, whitewater kayak ride that is thrilling and scary and joyful. Grace isn't merely an app to be acquired. It's an adventure to be lived.

Are you wondering what to make of this crazy existence? Too weary to have hope in yourself or your future? Worried you've messed up so badly that even God will turn you away? Wild grace is what you need.

Let's make certain it happens to you.

2

NO MORE CRITICS

A clean conscience. A clean record. A clean heart. Free from accusation. Free from condemnation. Not just from your past mistakes but also from the ones ahead.

You freely admit it. You're a social guy. It doesn't matter where the action is—you want to be in on it. Who wouldn't want to hang out with his best buddies on a Saturday night?

On this particular Saturday night, however, there's a problem. Your parents are out of town for the night, and you promised you'd stay home. Alone. As in you, yourself, and the family goldfish.

But then Drew calls. The movie's over, and the guys are looking for a place to chill. Nothing wild, just to hang out, play some Xbox, unwind. You know you should say no. You gave your word. But Drew can be persuasive, and he knows your parents are gone. Before you know it, you've invited five guys over.

Well, you think, *what's the harm? It'll be fun. My parents won't know the difference.*

Of course, when the guys arrive, it's not five people piling out of the cars but ten, a few of them girls. You have second thoughts, but you let them in anyway.

And it *is* fun. Jake tells a few jokes that get everybody going. Brandon does his always-hilarious impression of the school principal. Then Drew gives you the thumbs-up. You've just earned the top score on his social meter.

Now it's your turn to take center stage. You start the story of your climb up Mount Rainier last summer, the one where your partner slipped and you had to pull him back to safety. You build the suspense. You're getting to the good part. You can see that a couple of the girls are leaning forward, waiting to hear what happened.

This, you think, *is turning into a great party.*

Which is exactly when it happens. Headlights in the driveway. Car doors slamming. Front door opening.

Your parents are home early.

Busted.

Your spirits drop faster than your buddy on Mount Rainier. There are disappointed looks and angry words from your parents. But the worst part? Drew's muffled laugh as he walks out the door, shaking his head. Your score has just dropped from ten to zero.

I've been there. We all have. Sooner or later, we all get caught in the act. It's been going on forever. It happened even when Jesus walked the earth.

Picture a woman in bed, her sleep interrupted by voices.

"Get up, you harlot."

"What kind of woman do you think you are?"

Priests slammed open the bedroom door, threw back the window curtains, and pulled off the covers. Before she felt the warmth of the morning sun, the woman felt the heat of their scorn.

Sooner or later, we all get caught in the act.

"Shame on you."

"Pathetic."

"Disgusting."

She scarcely had time to cover her body before they marched her through the narrow streets. Dogs yelped. Roosters ran. Women leaned out their windows. Mothers snatched children off the path. Merchants peered out the doors of their shops. Jerusalem became a jury and announced its verdict with glares and crossed arms.

Then, as if the bedroom raid and parade of shame were inadequate, the men thrust her before the holiest judge of all.

"Teacher," they said to Jesus, "this woman was caught in the very act of adultery. The law of Moses says to stone her. What do you say?" (John 8:2–5 NLT).

There it is again—caught in the act. These pompous, proper authorities had their questions and convictions;

she had her flimsy nightgown and smeared lipstick. The woman had no exit. Deny the accusation? She'd been caught. Plead for mercy? From whom? From God? His spokesmen were squeezing stones and snarling their lips. No one would speak for her.

But someone would bend down for her.

Jesus "stooped down and wrote in the dust" (v. 6 NLT). We would expect him to stand up, step forward, or even ascend a stair and speak. But instead he leaned over. He descended lower than anyone else—beneath the priests, the people, even beneath the woman. The accusers looked down on her. To see Jesus, they had to look down even farther.

Grace is a God who stoops.

He does that. He bent down to wash feet, to embrace children. Bent down to pull Peter out of the sea, to pray in the garden before soldiers arrested him. Bent down to carry the cross they used to crucify him. Grace is a God who stoops. Here he stooped to write in the sand.

Remember the first occasion his fingers touched dirt? He scooped soil and formed Adam. As he touched the sun-baked soil beside the woman, Jesus may have been reliving the creation moment. Maybe Jesus wrote in the dirt for his own benefit. Or was it for hers? To divert gaping eyes from the barely dressed, just-caught woman who stood in the center of the circle?

The posse grew impatient with the silent, stooping Jesus. "They kept demanding an answer, so he stood up" (v. 7 NLT).

He lifted himself until his shoulders were straight and his head was high. He stood, not to preach, for his words would be few. Not for long, for he would soon bend down again. Not to instruct his followers; he didn't address them. He stood on behalf of the woman. He placed himself between her and the lynch mob and said, "'All right, stone her. But let those who have never sinned throw the first stones!' Then he stooped down again and wrote in the dust" (vv. 7–8 NLT).

Name-callers shut their mouths. Rocks fell to the ground. Jesus resumed his scribbling. "When the accusers heard this, they slipped away one by one, beginning with the oldest, until only Jesus was left in the middle of the crowd with the woman" (v. 9 NLT).

YOUR STORY:

Who are you more like, the posse with the pointing fingers or Jesus? Are you quick to accuse or quick to defend?

....

Have you ever, like this woman, been surrounded by an accusing crowd? How did that feel?

....

Jesus wasn't finished. He stood one final time and asked the woman, "Where are your accusers?" (v. 10 NLT).

My, my, my. What a question—not just for her but for us. Critical voices wake us up as well.

"You're stupid."

"Could you get any uglier?"

"You failed—again."

The voices in our world that judge and label us.

And the voices in our heads! Who is this rules cop who writes out a ticket every time we stumble? Who reminds us of every mistake? Does he ever shut up?

> Who is this rules cop who writes out a ticket every time we stumble?

No. Because Satan never shuts up. The apostle John called him the Accuser: "For the Accuser has been thrown down to earth—the one who accused our brothers and sisters before our God day and night" (Revelation 12:10 NLT). Day after day, hour after hour. The Accuser makes a career out of accusing. He has one aim: "to steal, and to kill, and to destroy" (John 10:10). Steal your peace, kill your dreams, and destroy your future.

The devil has signed up a crowd of silver-tongued demons to help him. He gets people to peddle his poison. Friends dredge up your past: "Remember that time you cheated on the test?" Preachers proclaim all guilt and no grace: "You don't measure up to God's standards." And parents, oh, your parents. They own a travel agency that specializes in guilt trips. They try to send you on one every day: "Why can't you grow up?" "Would it kill you to work a little harder?" "You could be so pretty. When are you going to lose a little weight?"

YOUR STORY:

Who does the Accuser use most often in your life? Parents? Teachers? Friends? You?

....

Taunts and put-downs. That's how Satan operates. He reminds you of your mistakes as often as you let him, marching you through the city streets and dragging your name through the mud. He pushes you into the center of the crowd and megaphones your sin:

THIS PERSON WAS CAUGHT IN THE ACT OF . . .

Cruelty. Stupidity. Dishonesty. Irresponsibility.

But he will not have the last word. Jesus has acted on your behalf.

He bent down. Low enough to sleep in a manger, work in a carpentry shop, sleep in a fishing boat. Low enough to rub shoulders with crooks and the diseased. Low enough to be spat upon, slapped, nailed, and speared. Low. Low enough to be buried.

And then he stood. Up from the slab of death. Upright in Joseph's tomb and right in Satan's face. Tall. High. He stood up for the woman and silenced her accusers, and he does the same for you. He stands up.

He "is in the presence of God at this very moment sticking up for us" (Romans 8:34 MSG). Let this sink in for a moment. In the presence of God, in defiance of Satan, Jesus Christ rises to your defense. He is the prince fighting off the attacking dragon. He is Aragorn protecting the hobbits with his sword.

Jesus offers a different road to your future. One with a clean conscience. A clean record. A clean heart. Free from accusation. Free from condemnation. Not just from your past mistakes but also from the ones ahead.

> Jesus overcomes the devil's guilt with words of grace.

"Since he will live forever, he will always be there to remind God that he has paid for [our] sins with his blood" (Hebrews 7:25 TLB). Christ forever stands in on your behalf.

Jesus overcomes the devil's guilt with words of grace.

You have been saved by God's grace. And he raised us up with Christ and gave us a seat with him in the heavens. He did this for those in Christ Jesus so that for all future time he could show the very great riches of his grace by being kind to us in Christ Jesus. (Ephesians 2:5–7 NCV)

This is what *grace* means: saved by God, raised by God, seated with God. You've heard the devil's insults and believed them. *Stupid. Lazy. Slow learner. Fast-talker. Quitter.* No longer. You are who your Creator says you are: *Spiritually alive. Connected to God. Awake to your potential. A billboard of mercy. An honored child.* This is the "aggressive forgiveness we call *grace*" (Romans 5:20 MSG, emphasis mine).

A young man named Josh Phillips can tell you about it.

IF ANYBODY KNEW THE REAL ME

by Josh Phillips as told to Ann Swindell

Ann, a girl in one of my high school classes, was inviting me to a Wednesday night Bible study with some of her friends. Something inside told me to say, "No way." Something else told me to give it a try.

"What do you guys do there?" I mumbled.

"We eat dinner and read the Bible. It's pretty laid-back, but we talk about God a lot."

"I'm not into the whole 'God thing,'" I said

indifferently. "But is dinner free?" I figured I wouldn't go if it cost me.

"Yes, it's free," Ann said with a laugh. "So is the fun."

She was right. The food was free and good, and the study turned out to be fun. I couldn't figure out how people could laugh so much while reading the Bible. But they did. So, along with going to church, I also attended the Bible study for the rest of my junior year. Hanging out with Ann and her friends was better than constantly trying to pick up girls. It felt like I had a group of good, genuine friends for the first time ever.

But I had a problem I was afraid to discuss. The more I studied the Bible with my church friends, the more I realized how bad I was. I'd discovered God didn't want people to have pre-marital sex, and I'd sure broken that rule. And I knew God didn't want people to be full of them-selves. Guilty again, especially when it came to wrestling, a sport I excelled in.

While I was trying to be a better person, my life was still one big mess. *If anybody knew the real me*, I thought, *they wouldn't want me around.*

"Ann, you're perfect, and so is everyone else at church," I said as I stared downward. "And I'm so bad."

I was sitting next to Ann during the noon meal at a Christian camp. A couple of months before summer break, she'd encouraged me to sign up for the weeklong retreat. And I'd been having a great time, but around midweek I couldn't stand it any longer. So I spilled my guts. I figured Ann was about to tell me I didn't have a chance with God.

"Josh, you are guilty of sin," she said softly.

I knew it. I'm so toast.

"But so am I."

"Are you kidding?" I blurted out. "I bet you've never sinned in your life!"

Ann laughed and then said, "You'd be betting wrong. We're all sinners and we've all messed up. That's why we need Jesus. He's the only one who didn't sin and he's the only one who can save us from our sin."

"But you don't know all of the bad stuff I've done. Especially when it comes to girls. I—I've done things I don't even want to talk about, they're so bad."

Ann answered, "What's your point? Jesus still loves you no matter what you've done. He can save you if you believe in him."

Something inside of me broke, and I felt tears burning in my eyes. I didn't cry, but it was the closest I'd come since I was little kid. "Ann," I said with my voice shaking, "I want Jesus to save me."

Several months after becoming a Christian, I stood on a podium with a gold medal hanging around my neck. With God's help and a lot of practice, I'd won the state wrestling championship for my weight class. I was proud and happy.

But that didn't even compare to the prize I'd already won with Ann's help. Though I knew I was far from perfect, I didn't feel bad anymore. I had the forgiveness and love of Jesus. And *that*, I knew, was a victory truly worth celebrating.[1]

Josh Phillips replaced guilt with grace. When grace happens, Satan's accusations sputter and fall like a deflated balloon.

So why do we still hear them? Why do we, as Christians, still feel guilt?

Maybe it's because not all guilt is bad. God uses

appropriate doses of guilt to awaken us to mistakes that offend him. We know guilt is God-given when it causes "indignation . . . alarm . . . longing . . . concern . . . readiness to see justice done" (2 Corinthians 7:11 NIV).

God's guilt brings enough regret to change us. Satan's guilt brings enough regret to enslave us. Don't let him lock you in chains. Remember, when God looks at you, he sees Jesus first. It boils down to this choice: do you trust your Advocate or your Accuser?

Your answer has serious implications. It did for Jean Valjean. Victor Hugo introduced us to this character in his classic novel *Les Misérables*. Valjean enters the pages as a vagabond, a just-released prisoner wearing threadbare trousers and a tattered jacket. Nineteen years in a French prison have left him rough and fearless. He's walked for four days in the Alpine chill of nineteenth-century France, only to find that no inn will take him, no tavern will feed him. Finally he knocks on the door of a bishop's house.

Monseigneur Myriel is seventy-five years old. Like Valjean, he has lost much. The only valuables he has left are some silverware, a soup ladle, and two candlesticks. Valjean tells his story and expects the religious man to turn him away. But the bishop is kind. He asks the visitor to sit near a fire. "You did not need to tell me who you were," he explains. "This is not my house—it is the house of Jesus Christ."[2]

After some time the bishop takes the ex-convict to the table, where they dine on soup and bread, figs, and cheese with wine, using the bishop's fine silverware.

He shows Valjean to a bedroom. In spite of the comfort, the ex-prisoner can't sleep. In spite of the kindness of the bishop, he can't resist the temptation. He stuffs the silverware into his knapsack. The priest sleeps through the robbery, and Valjean runs into the night.

But he doesn't get far. The policemen catch him and march him back to the bishop's house. Valjean knows what his capture means—prison for the rest of his life. But then something wonderful happens. Before the officer can explain the crime, the bishop steps forward.

> God will never, never, never let us down if we have faith and put our trust in Him.
>
> —Mother Teresa

"Oh! Here you are! I'm so glad to see you. I can't believe you forgot the candlesticks! They are made of pure silver as well. . . . Please take them with the forks and spoons I gave you."

Valjean is stunned. The bishop dismisses the policemen and then turns and says, "Jean Valjean, my brother, you no longer belong to evil, but to good. I have bought your soul from you. I take it back from evil thoughts and deeds and the Spirit of Hell, and I give it to God."[3]

Valjean has a choice: believe the priest or believe his past. Jean Valjean believes the priest. He becomes the mayor of a small town. He builds a factory and gives jobs to the poor. He takes pity on a dying mother and raises her daughter.

Grace changed him. Let it change you. Reject Satan's voice. You "have an Advocate with the Father, Jesus Christ the righteous" (1 John 2:1). As your Advocate, he defends you and says on your behalf, "There is therefore now no condemnation to those who are in Christ Jesus" (Romans 8:1). Take that, Satan!

Wasn't this the message of Jesus to the woman?

"Where are your accusers? Didn't even one of them condemn you?"

"No, Lord," she said.

And Jesus said, "Neither do I. Go and sin no more." (John 8:10–11 NLT)

Within a few moments the courtyard was empty. Jesus, the woman, her critics—they all left. But let's stay a little longer. Look at the rocks on the ground, abandoned and unused. And look at the scribbling in the sand. It's the only sermon Jesus ever wrote. Although we don't know the words, I'm wondering if they read like this:

Grace happens here.

3

THE BEST
TRADE YOU'LL
EVER MAKE

We won't appreciate what grace does
until we understand who we are. We are
rebels. We are Barabbas. Like him, we
deserve to die.

The jail cell of Barabbas contains a single square window about the size of a face. Barabbas looked through it once and only once. When he saw the execution hill, he lowered himself to the floor, leaned against the wall, and pulled his knees to his chest. That was an hour ago. He hasn't moved since.

He hasn't spoken since.

Odd for him. Barabbas has been a man of many words. When the guards came at sunrise to transfer him out of the barracks, he boasted that he would be a free man before noon. On the way to the cell, he cursed the soldiers and mocked their Caesar.

But since arriving, he hasn't uttered a sound. No person to speak to, for one thing. Nothing to say, for another. For all his brave talk, he knows he'll be crucified by noon, dead by sundown. What is there to say? He has no chests of treasure, no fertile lands, no friends in high places. He has nothing to trade for his life. He knows what awaits him.

A few hundred yards away from his small cell, a not-so-small gathering of men murmurs in disapproval. Religious leaders mostly. A cluster of beards and robes and stern faces. Tired and angry. On the steps above them stand a refined Roman and a grubby Galilean. The first man gestures to the second and appeals to the crowd.

"You brought me this man as one who was inciting the people to rebellion. I have examined him in your presence and have found no basis for your charges against him. Neither has Herod, for he sent him back to us; as you can see, he has done nothing to deserve death. Therefore, I will punish him and then release him."

With one voice they cried out, "Away with this man! Release Barabbas to us!" (Barabbas had been thrown into prison for an insurrection in the city, and for murder.) (Luke 23:14–19 NIV)

That last sentence explains Barabbas: rebel and murderer. Anger in his heart and blood on his hands. Defiant. Violent. A troublemaker. A life taker. He is guilty and proud of it. Is Pilate, the Roman governor, supposed to treat such a man with grace? The crowd thinks so. Moreover, they want Pilate to execute Jesus instead, a man whom Pilate declares has "done nothing to deserve death."

Pilate is no friend of Jesus. The Galilean means nothing to him. If Jesus is guilty, let him pay for his crime. The governor is willing to crucify a guilty man. But an innocent one?

"I DIDN'T DO IT"

Have you ever been accused of something you didn't do? How about thrown in jail for it?

Cody Webb has.

In March 2007, Cody was a sophomore at Pennsylvania's Hempfield Area High School. The fifteen-year-old was an honor student who'd never served a minute in detention. But his good-guy rep took a serious hit when police officers drove up to the school, handcuffed Cody in front of busloads of students, and led him away. Cody spent twelve days locked up in a juvenile detention center.

What was Cody's crime? He'd called the school's hotline during the night to see if there would be a weather-related delay in the morning. Police and school officials said that the call was a bomb threat. Cody said he was innocent.

Many days later, the confusion was cleared up when someone discovered that the device recording the time of phone calls to the school had not been reset to daylight saving time. According to cell phone records and the adjusted school time, Cody's call was actually made more than an hour earlier than the bomb call.

Cody never backed down during his traumatic experience. "I wasn't going to admit to something I didn't do," he said. "Me and God know I didn't do it."[1]

Innocent. Accused. Arrested. Punished and scorned for a crime he didn't commit.

Jesus understands.

Back in Jerusalem, Pilate must decide what to do with this Jesus. He knows the man doesn't deserve to die. Maybe a lecture, even a lashing. But not the cross. Pilate makes no fewer than four attempts to release Jesus. He tells the Jews to settle the matter (John 18:28–31). He refers the issue to Herod (Luke 23:4–7). He tries to persuade the Jews to accept Jesus as the prisoner released at Passover (Mark 15:6–10). He offers a compromise: whipping instead of execution (Luke 23:22). He does all he can to release Jesus. Why? "I find no fault in Him at all" (John 18:38).

With these words, the governor unintentionally steps into the sandals of spiritual teacher. He states first what Paul would record later: Jesus "knew no sin" (2 Corinthians 5:21). Of equal ranking with Jesus' water walking, dead raising, and disease healing is this skyscraper-tall truth: he never sinned. It's not that Jesus could not sin but that he did not. He could have broken bread with the devil in the wilderness or broken ranks with his Father in Gethsemane. "[He] was in all points tempted as we are, yet without sin" (Hebrews 4:15).

Jesus was God's model of a human being. Ever honest among hypocrites. Relentlessly kind in a world of cruelty. Heaven-focused despite countless distractions. It's not just that Jesus passed every test. He posted a perfect score on every test.

> Jesus was God's model of a human being.

Can you imagine such a life? Can you say the same about yours? No mistakes? Never a rude comment? Not a single red mark on your essays? I can't say that. Neither could a high school student named Steve Farrar.

For his sophomore year, Steve's family moved to a new town. He didn't know a soul at his new school. Steve figured that going out for a sport would be a great way to make friends. He could get to know more guys in three days of playing ball than in three months of classes.

Steve was a good basketball player and wished he could try out for the varsity team. But he'd messed up. His report card carried a bad mark. He'd earned a D in a class. It was his own fault.

He'd goofed off and hadn't turned in all his papers on time. It was a short-term teen rebellion, but now he would pay the price.

Fortunately for Steve, school rules allowed a student to play sports if he had just one D. Unfortunately for Steve, his dad had his own eligibility rules. If one of his kids scored below a C, he couldn't play ball. Simple. And as unchangeable as a final score.

It wasn't that Steve's dad didn't want him on the court. He was all for it. He'd been all-state in both basketball and football in high school, went to college on a basketball scholarship, and was even offered a contract to play football for the Pittsburgh Steelers. He understood how great athletics can be. But this dad preferred developing Steve's character over his jump shot. Steve knew his academic mini-revolt fell short of his dad's standards. He had a father who paid attention to such things. So do we.

It's not that God doesn't want us to enjoy life. He's all for it. He created us for it. But when we decide that we're in charge, he doesn't let it slide. There are consequences. He lets us face the misery that comes from our mistakes. He prefers that we learn to follow his amazing plan instead of flounder with our own.

YOUR STORY:

How do you feel about the bad marks in your life? Guilty? Or do you think they're not as bad as some people's, so they're no big deal?

....

How do you think God feels about them?

....

Back at school, Steve Farrar was getting the message. He worked harder in class, and he at least was allowed to play hoops in PE class. One day the varsity basketball coach watched. The more times Steve scored, the more excited the coach got. His future was suddenly in focus. Victories. Championships. Cheesy TV commercials. After class, the coach asked Steve why he hadn't tried out for the varsity team. Steve explained about his bad grade and his dad's rule and said he'd try out the next year.

The coach was a big, aggressive guy. He was used to getting his way. "What's your phone number?" the coach asked. "I'm going to call your dad."

"I'll be happy to give you the phone number," Steve said, "but it will be a waste of your time."

The next morning the coach approached Steve in the locker room. "I talked to your dad yesterday afternoon, and he wouldn't budge. I explained the school eligibility rules, but he wouldn't change his mind. I don't have much respect for your father."

Steve couldn't believe his ears. This coach didn't respect his father? Even Steve had enough sense to know that his dad was doing the right thing.

"Coach," Steve said, "I can tell you that I highly respect my dad. And I also want you to know that I will never play basketball for you."

Steve never did. He got his grades up but never went out for varsity basketball. He couldn't play for a man who didn't respect the standards of a loving father.[2]

Aren't we, though, a lot like that basketball coach? We're okay for a while with letting God pick the players and diagram the plays, but when something "better" catches our eye—the in-crowd friend, the creative-but-crude movie, that cute girl or guy—we take the whistle and clipboard. We make up our own rules.

The problem is that unlike Jesus, we're not faultless. We're fault-filled. And right near the top is our desire to be in control. We want things our own way. Even when we try to do right, sooner or later we end up blowing it again. An insult slips off the tongue. A promise is put on the shelf. A relationship is fouled, a class failed. And God is left behind, forgotten more quickly than yesterday's homework.

You and I are world-class rebels.

Where does it leave us? Stuck in the same cell with Barabbas. We're like him. We *are* him. Sinners. Rebels. Murderers.

Am I overstating the case? I don't think so. It doesn't matter if we've literally killed someone. The point is that we are rebels against God. We shout, "God, I don't want you to be my king! I want a kingless kingdom! Even better, a kingdom in which *I* am king!" We stage a revolution.

We storm God's castle, put on his crown, and sit on his throne. We roar, "I want to run my own life, thank you very much!" We tell God to get out, get lost, and not come back. You and I are world-class rebels. So is every single person who has taken a breath.

A REBEL NAMED ROBERT

by Dr. James Dobson

Robert was a rebel. He was also ten years old. He ruled by means of blackmail. If he and his mother were in public and she dared say no to something Robert wanted, he threatened to take his clothes off. His mother, afraid of causing a scene, always gave in.

Thanks to this threat, Robert had been in charge his whole life. Then he met his match—a wise old dentist.

At his appointment, Robert was asked to sit in the patient chair. He refused, saying he'd take his clothes off if the dentist made him sit. After all, it had always worked before.

"Son," the dentist said, "take 'em off."

Robert did just that. Then he got in the chair,

naked, and cooperated for the rest of his visit. When cavities had been drilled and filled, Robert said, "Give me my clothes back now."

"I'm sorry," the dentist said. "Tell your mother that we're going to keep your clothes tonight." An embarrassed Robert, wearing not even a hat, was forced to walk through a waiting room filled with giggling patients.

The next day Robert's mother came to retrieve his clothes—and to thank the dentist. "You are the first person to call his bluff, Doctor," she said. "The impact on Robert has been incredible!"[3]

Robert had hoped to rule for a lifetime, but his dictatorship died in a dentist's chair. He was left with nothing—in more ways than one. It's a lesson for every would-be rebel to remember.

Like Robert, we all rebel. The Bible puts it in plain language: "We all, like sheep, have gone astray, each of us has turned to his own way" (Isaiah 53:6 NIV). Your way may be ignoring homework, my way may be ignoring other people, another person's way might be bragging or gossiping or drinking, but every person has tried to go his or her way without God. It is not that some of us have rebelled. We all have. "There is no one righteous, not even one; there is no one who understands, no one who seeks God. All have turned away, they have together become worthless; there is no one who does good, not even one" (Romans 3:10–12 NIV).

This isn't news we want to hear. It's a text we'd rather delete. But it's truth. To get to the good stuff—grace—we first have to accept that we're neck-deep in the bad stuff called sin.

We won't appreciate what grace does until we understand who we are. We are rebels. We are Barabbas. Like him, we deserve to die. Four prison walls, thickened with fear, hurt, and hate, surround us. We are in jail because of our past, our low-road choices, and our high-minded pride. We have been found guilty. And we have nothing to offer in trade for our lives.

We sit on the floor of the dusty cell, awaiting the final moment. Our executioner's footsteps echo against stone walls. Head between knees, we don't look up as he opens the door; we don't lift our eyes as he begins to speak. We know what he is going to say. "Time to pay up." But we hear something else.

"You're free to go. They took Jesus instead of you."

The door swings open, the guard barks, "Get out," and we find ourselves in the light of the morning sun, shackles gone, crimes pardoned, wondering, *What just happened?*

Grace happened.

Christ took away your sins. Where did he take them? To the top of a hill called Calvary, where he endured not just the nails of the Romans, the mockery of the crowd, and the spear of the soldier but also the anger of God.

> Jesus took your punishment, and God gave you credit for Jesus' perfection.

Fill your heart with this, the finest summary of God's greatest accomplishment:

> God in his gracious kindness declares us not guilty. He has done this through Christ Jesus, who has freed us by taking away our sins. *For God sent Jesus to take the punishment for our sins* and to satisfy God's anger against us. We are made right with God when we believe that Jesus shed his blood, sacrificing his life for us. (Romans 3:24–25 NLT, emphasis mine)

God didn't overlook your sins; he won't endorse them. He didn't punish you; he won't destroy you. He instead found a way to punish the sin and preserve the sinner. Jesus took your punishment, and God gave you credit for

Jesus' perfection.

It's the best trade you'll ever make.

We are not told how the first Barabbas responded to the gift of freedom. Maybe he scorned it out of pride or refused it out of shame. We don't know. But you can determine what to do with yours. Personalize it.

As long as the cross is God's gift to the world, it will touch you but not change you. Satisfying as it is to shout, "Christ died for the world!" even sweeter it is to whisper, "Christ died for *me*."

"For *my* sins he died."

"He took *my* place on the cross."

"He carried *my* sins, *my* cold and cruel heart."

"Through the cross he claimed, cleansed, and called *me*."

"He felt *my* shame and spoke *my* name."

Be the Barabbas who says, "Thank you." Thank God for the day grace happened to you. Thank Jesus for giving his life for yours—the best trade you'll ever make.

4

GRACE IS
ALL WE NEED

His grace is not a gentle shower washing
away the problem. It is a raging, roaring
river whose current knocks you off your feet
and carries you into the presence of God.

Heather Sample suspected trouble the moment she saw the cut on her dad's hand. The two had sat down for a quick lunch between surgical procedures. Heather spotted the wound and asked him about it. When Kyle explained that the injury had happened during an operation, she suddenly felt sick to her stomach.

Both were doctors. Both understood the danger of treating AIDS patients in Zimbabwe. The virus could spread through contact with a patient's blood. It destroyed the immune system. It was incurable.

And now one of them had been exposed.

Kyle Sheets was a twelve-year veteran of medical mission trips. I knew Kyle when I was a college student. He married a delightful girl named Bernita and settled down in a small Texas town to raise a family and treat the needy. Turns out, they raised a family that treats the needy. Ten children in all. Each involved in works of compassion. As founder and chairman of Physicians Aiding Physicians Abroad, Kyle spent several weeks a year working in mission hospitals in developing countries. This trip to Zimbabwe was not his first.

Exposure to the AIDS virus was.

Heather urged her father to begin the antiretroviral treatment immediately in order to prevent HIV infection. Kyle was reluctant. He knew the side effects. Each was life threatening. Still, Heather insisted, and he consented. Within hours he was violently ill.

Nausea, fever, and weakness were only the initial signs that something was terribly wrong. For ten days Kyle continued to worsen. Then he broke out in the unmistakable rash of Stevens-Johnson syndrome, which is almost always fatal. They moved up their date for returning to the States and began to wonder if Kyle would survive the forty-hour trip, which included a twelve-hour layover in South Africa and a seventeen-hour flight to Atlanta.

Kyle boarded the plane with a 104.5-degree fever. He shook with chills. By this time he was having trouble breathing and was unable to sit up. Incoherent. Eyes yellowed. Liver enlarged and painful. Both doctors recognized the symptoms of acute liver failure. Heather felt the full weight of her father's life on her shoulders.

> Heather felt the full weight of her father's life on her shoulders.

Heather explained the situation to the pilots and convinced them that her dad's best hope was the fastest flight possible to the United States. Having only a stethoscope and a vial of heart medicine, she took her seat next to his and wondered how she would pull his body into the aisle to do CPR if his heart stopped.

Several minutes into the flight, Kyle drifted off to sleep. Heather crawled over him and made it to the bathroom in time to vomit the water she had just drunk. She slumped on the floor in a fetal position, wept, and prayed, *I need help.*

YOUR STORY:

Where or who do you turn to when you're in trouble?

....

What do you most need help with right now? Have you talked to God about it?

....

Heather doesn't remember how long she prayed, but it was long enough for a concerned passenger to knock on the door. She opened it to see four men standing in the galley. One asked if she was okay. Heather assured him that she was fine and told him that she was a doctor. His face brightened as he explained that he and his three friends were physicians too. "And so are ninety-six other passengers!" he said.

The plane could have been filled with conference-bound circus jugglers. Or tattoo artists. Or professional whistlers. But no, Heather and her dad "happened" to be on a flight with one hundred physicians from Mexico.

Heather explained the situation and asked for the doctors' help and prayers. They gave both. They alerted a colleague who was a top-rank infectious disease doctor. Together they evaluated Kyle's condition and agreed that nothing else could be done.

They offered to watch him so Heather could rest. She did. When she awoke, Kyle was standing and talking to one of the doctors. Although still emergency room–level sick, he was much stronger. Heather began to recognize God's hand at work. He had placed them on exactly the right plane with exactly the right people. God had met their need with grace.

He'll meet yours as well. Perhaps your journey is difficult. You are Heather on the flight, watching a loved one struggle. Or you are Kyle Sheets, feeling the rage of disease and death in your body. Maybe you're failing a class or a friend. You're so overwhelmed you don't think you can face one more day.

You are fearful and weak, but you are not alone. The words of "Amazing Grace" are yours.

> You are fearful and weak, but you are not alone.

Although written in the 1700s, they bring hope like today's sunrise. "'Tis grace hath brought me safe thus far, and grace will lead me home."[1] You have his Spirit within you. Heavenly hosts above you. Jesus Christ standing up for you. You have God's super-powered grace to strengthen and carry you through.

Paul's life revealed this truth. He wrote, "I was given a thorn in my flesh, a messenger from Satan to torment me and keep me from becoming proud. Three different times

I begged the Lord to take it away. Each time he said, 'My grace is all you need. My power works best in weakness'" (2 Corinthians 12:7–9 NLT).

A thorn in the flesh. Such vivid imagery. The sharp end of a thorn pierces the soft skin of life and lodges beneath the surface. Every step is a reminder of the thorn in the flesh.

The disease in the body.

The sadness in the heart.

The sister in the rehab center.

The dad moving out.

The D on the report card.

The craving to be one of the cool crowd.

The tears in the middle of the night.

The thorn in the flesh.

"Take it away," you've pleaded. Not once, twice, or even three times. You've outprayed Paul. He prayed a sprint; you've prayed the Boston Marathon. And you're about to hit the wall at mile nineteen. This wound oozes pain, and you see no sign of tweezers coming from heaven. But what you hear is this: "My grace is all you need."

God's great grace wipes out everything else on the landscape. It is not puny but plentiful. Not teeny but torrential. Not mini but majestic. It meets us right now, at our point of need, and equips us with courage, wisdom, and

> God's great grace wipes out everything else on the landscape.

strength. It surprises us in our worst moment with overflowing buckets of faith. His grace is not a gentle shower washing away the problem. It is a raging, roaring river whose current knocks you off your feet and carries you into the presence of God.

Kim Meeder was carried in that current just when she needed it most.

HE NEVER LETS GO

by Kim Meeder

I was nine years old when the inconceivable happened. Divorce was tearing our family apart. Distraught, my dad sought help in professional counseling and medication. Tragically, the help he so desperately needed was not to be found.

One day a friend of my father's picked up my sisters and me from school and took us to our grandparents' house. No one spoke. During that drive I knew something catastrophic had happened. At my grandparents' house a distressed woman tried to comfort me in her arms. She kept repeating, "I'm sorry. I'm sorry. I'm so deeply sorry." Finally she blurted out, "Your father has just murdered your mother and killed himself."

My first thought was that she was a liar. She *had* to be a liar because what she said simply could not be true.

I tore away and burst out the house's back door. I ran and ran through a small orchard until I fell, facedown, in the powdery, dry earth. I heard screaming and realized it was coming from me.

"Jesus, help me!" I cried. "Help me!"

And then, He did.

I didn't really know who Jesus was. I'd been to church only a few times in my life. Yet in that moment of despair, I somehow knew He was the only safe direction I could turn and if I didn't, I would die.

What I understand now is how on that terrible day the Lord of all creation came and knelt in the dirt beside a breaking child. He reached down and took the small hand that reached up to Him . . . and He has *never* let go.

Only through His grace did I begin picking up the pieces of my shattered life. My sisters and I moved in with my grandparents and started attending church. In the years that followed, I learned that Jesus was my Redeemer and my shelter. Despite the grief and despair I faced, I always found comfort in Him.[2]

God is merciful to us—and so much more. Grace goes beyond mercy. Mercy gave the prodigal son a second chance. Grace threw him a party. Mercy prompted the Good Samaritan to bandage the wounds of the victim. Grace prompted him to leave his credit card as payment for the victim's care. Mercy forgave the thief on the cross. Grace escorted him into paradise. Mercy pardons us. Grace empowers us. And according to Paul, God's grace is all we need to meet every single challenge of our lives.

All we need. Sounds too good to be true, doesn't it? Don't we secretly fear his grace is going to run out when we need it most? Like when we're starving and the cafeteria lunch lady hands the last slice of pizza to the guy ahead of us in line. Like when we're online, trying to order tickets to the concert we're dying to see, and the screen fills with the words "Sold Out."

Can God run out of grace?

Plunge a sponge into Lake Erie. Did you absorb every drop? Take a deep breath. Did you suck the oxygen out of the atmosphere? Pluck a pine needle from a tree in Yosemite. Did you wipe out the forest's foliage? Watch an ocean wave crash against the beach. Will there never be another?

Of course there will. No sooner will one wave crash into the sand than another appears. Then another, then another. This is a picture of God's never-ending grace. *Grace* is simply another word for his tumbling, rumbling reservoir of strength and protection. It comes at us not in occasional drips but in titanic torrents, wave upon wave. We've barely regained our balance from one breaker, and then, *bam*, here comes another.

"Grace upon grace" (John 1:16 NASB). We dare to stake our hope on the gladdest news of all: if God permits the challenge, he will provide the grace to meet it.

We never exhaust his supply. "Stop asking so much! My grace reservoir is running dry." Heaven knows no such words. God has enough grace to solve every dilemma you face, wipe every tear you cry, and answer every question you ask.

> Grace is simply another word for God's tumbling, rumbling reservoir of strength and protection.

Would we expect anything less from God? Would he send his Son to die for us and not send his power to sustain us? Paul found such logic impossible. "He who did not spare his own Son, but gave him up for us all—how will he not also, along with him, graciously give us all things?" (Romans 8:32 NIV).

Take all your worries to the Man on the cross, Paul urged. Stand in the shadow of God's crucified Son. Now pose your questions. *Is Jesus on my side?* Look at the wound in his. *Will he stay with me?* Having given the supreme and costliest gift, "how can he fail to lavish upon us all he has to give?" (Romans 8:32 NEB).

Let God's grace drown your fears. Anxiety still comes, for certain. Dating. Drugs. Disease. Divorce. Pressure from parents, from teachers, from friends. Problems make up your world. But they don't control it! Grace does. God has surrounded you with a fleet of angels to meet your needs in his way at the right time.

With the help of those one hundred doctors, my friend Kyle survived the flight to America and recovered from the reaction. Tests show no trace of HIV. He and Heather resumed their practices with renewed conviction of God's protection. When I asked Kyle about the experience, he reflected that on three other occasions he has heard an airline attendant ask, "Is there a doctor on board?" In each instance Kyle was the only physician on the flight.

"As Heather wheeled me onto the plane, I wondered if anyone would be on board to help us." God, he soon discovered, answered his prayer a hundred times over.

He stands ready to do the same for you.

PART 2

GRACE
IN
ACTION

5

RICH WITH GRACE

When grace happens, generosity happens. Unsquashable, eye-popping bigheartedness happens.

my Wells knew her bridal shop would be busy. Brides-to-be took full advantage of the days right after Thanksgiving. It was common for families to spend the better part of the holiday weekend looking at wedding dresses in her San Antonio, Texas, store. Amy was prepared to give service to shoppers. She never expected to give grace to a dying man.

Across town Jack Autry was in the hospital, struggling to stay alive. He was in the final stages of cancer. He had collapsed two days before and had been rushed to the emergency room. His extended family was in town not just to celebrate Thanksgiving together but to make preparations for his daughter's wedding. Chrysalis was only months from marriage. The women in the family had planned to spend the day selecting a wedding gown. But now with Jack in the hospital, Chrysalis didn't want to go.

Jack insisted. After much persuasion Chrysalis, her mother, her future mother-in-law, and her sisters went to the bridal salon. The shop owner noticed the women were a bit subdued, but she assumed this was just a quiet family. She helped Chrysalis try on dress after dress until she found an ivory duchess silk and satin gown that everyone loved. Jack was fond of calling Chrysalis his princess, and the dress, Chrysalis commented, made her look just like one.

That's when Amy heard about Jack. Because of the cancer, he couldn't come see his daughter in her dress.

And because of the medical bills, the family couldn't buy the dress yet. It appeared that Jack Autry would die without seeing his daughter dressed as a bride.

Amy would hear nothing of it. She told Chrysalis to take the gown and veil to the hospital and wear it for her daddy. Amy says, "I knew it was fine. There was no doubt in my mind to do this. God was talking to me." No credit card was requested or given. Amy didn't even make note of a phone number. She urged the family to go directly to the hospital. Chrysalis didn't have to be told twice.

When she arrived at her father's room, he was heavily medicated and asleep. As family members woke him, the doors to the room slowly opened, and there he saw his daughter, engulfed in fifteen yards of layered, billowing silk. He was able to stay alert for about twenty seconds.

"But those twenty seconds were magical," Chrysalis remembers. "My daddy saw me walk in wearing the most beautiful dress. He was really weak. He smiled and just kept looking at me. I held his hand, and he held mine. I asked him if I looked like a princess. . . . He nodded. He looked at me a little more, and it almost looked like he was about to cry. And then he went to sleep."

Three days later he died.[1]

Chrysalis and her family couldn't afford to give Jack one last vision of his daughter dressed as a princess. Yet thanks to Amy's generosity, they grew rich in a moment of abundant, cascading grace.

God to Amy to Chrysalis to Jack. Isn't this how grace works?

Isn't this how God works? He starts the process. He doesn't just love; he *lavishes* us with love (1 John 3:1 NIV). He doesn't dole out wisdom; he "gives generously to all without finding fault" (James 1:5 NIV). He is rich in "kindness, tolerance and patience" (Romans 2:4 NIV). His grace is "exceedingly abundant" (1 Timothy 1:14) and "indescribable" (2 Corinthians 9:14–15).

> God doesn't just love; he lavishes us with love.

He turned a few bread loaves and fish into food for five thousand, changed water at a wedding into wine, and overflowed the boat of Peter with fish, twice. He healed all who sought health, taught all who wanted instruction, and saved all who accepted the gift of salvation.

God "supplies seed to the sower and bread for food" (2 Corinthians 9:10 NIV). The Greek verb for "supplies" (*epichoregeo*) pulls back the curtain on God's generosity. It combines "dance" (*choros*) with the verb "to lead" (*hegeomai*).[2] It literally means "to lead a dance." Picture him at the center of the circle, a huge smile on his face, teaching you the latest dance step. When God gives, he dances for joy. He strikes up the band and leads the giving parade.

He loves to give.

God even promises a whopping reward for joining and

giving with him. Peter asked Jesus, "We left everything and followed you. What do we get out of it?" (Matthew 19:27 MSG). Seems like a good chance for Jesus to adjust Peter's "Me first" attitude. He didn't. Instead, he assured Peter, along with all disciples, that we "will get it all back a hundred times over, not to mention the considerable bonus of eternal life" (Matthew 19:29 MSG). We might call that generous.

"So don't be afraid, little flock. For it gives your Father great happiness to give you the Kingdom."

—Luke 12:32 (NLT)

God dispenses his goodness not with an eyedropper but a fire hydrant. Your heart is a Dixie cup, and his grace is the Mediterranean Sea. You simply can't contain it all. So let it bubble over. Spill out. Pour forth. And enjoy the flood.

It is the Lord's unending flow of grace that allows him to give so completely and to keep on giving. When we accept his grace, we also link to his everlasting supply. Our reaction should be to give in turn to others—our time, our money, our things, our wisdom, our love.

When grace happens, generosity happens. Unsquashable, eye-popping bigheartedness happens.

It certainly happened to Zacchaeus. If the New Testament has a con artist, this is the man. He never met a person he couldn't swindle or saw a dollar he couldn't hustle. He was a "chief tax collector" (Luke 19:2). First-century tax collectors cheated anything that walked. The Roman government allowed them to keep all they could take. Zacchaeus took a lot. "He was rich" (v. 2). Tailored-suit-and-manicured-nails rich. Cruise-around-town-in-a-convertible rich. Spring-break-in-the-Bahamas rich. Filthy rich.

And guilty rich? He wouldn't be the first crook to feel regrets. And he wouldn't be the first to wonder if Jesus could help him shake them. Maybe that's how he ended up in the tree. When Jesus and his followers traveled through Jericho, half the city showed up to take a look. Men, women, and children on both sides of the street jostled for curbside views, Zacchaeus among them. But citizens of Jericho weren't about to let short-in-stature, long-on-enemies Zacchaeus elbow his way to the front of the crowd. He was left hopping up and down behind the wall of people, hoping to get a glimpse.

> For grace is given not because we have done good works, but in order that we may be able to do them.
>
> —Augustine

That's when he spotted the sycamore, shimmied up, and scurried out. He was happy to go out on a limb to get a good look at Christ. He never imagined that Christ would take a good look at him. But Jesus did. "Zacchaeus, come down immediately. I must stay at your house today" (v. 5 NIV).

The pint-sized petty thief looked to one side, then the other, in case another Zacchaeus was in the tree. Turns out, Jesus was talking to him. To him! Of all the homes in town, Jesus selected Zack's. Financed with illegal money, avoided by neighbors, yet on that day it was graced by the presence of Jesus.

> Grace changed the tax collector's heart. Is grace changing yours?

Zacchaeus was never quite the same. "Look, Lord! Here and now I give half of my possessions to the poor, and if I have cheated anybody out of anything, I will pay back four times the amount" (v. 8 NIV). Suddenly, Zacchaeus owned a different kind of wealth. Not the kind marked by piles of bills and coins but by deeds of generosity and love.

Despite Zacchaeus's bad choices, despite his dishonest past, Jesus offered him kindness and a seat at heaven's table. Jesus offered him grace. And when that grace walked in the front door, selfishness scampered out the back. It changed the tax collector's heart.

Is grace changing yours?

YOUR STORY:

How has God given you grace lately?

....

How have you passed on that grace to someone else?

....

Unlike Zacchaeus, some people resist the change. The ungrateful servant did (Matthew 18:23–35). In the story Jesus told, the servant owed more money to the king than he could ever repay. Try as he might, the man couldn't make the payments. He'd sooner find an iPod in his cereal than he'd find cash for the debt. "So the king ordered that he, his wife, his children, and everything he had be sold to pay the debt. But the man fell down before the king and begged him, 'Oh, sir, be patient with me, and I will pay it all.' Then the king was filled with pity for him, and he released him and forgave his debt" (vv. 25–27 NLT).

The man hurried to the house of a person who owed him a few dollars. You would expect the just-blessed man to be quick to bless, right? Not in this case. He demanded payment. He turned a deaf ear to the fellow's pleas for mercy and locked him in debtors' prison. How could he be so coldhearted? Jesus doesn't tell us. He leaves us to speculate, and I speculate this much: grace never happened to him. He thought he had beaten the system. Instead of leaving the king's castle with a thankful heart ("What a great king I serve!"), he left with a puffed-with-pride chest ("What a clever man I am!"). The king learned of the self-centered response and went ballistic. "You evil servant! I forgave you that tremendous debt because you pleaded with me. Shouldn't you have mercy on your fellow servant, just as I had mercy on you?" (vv. 32–33 NLT).

> The self-centered servant didn't get it. The grace-given give grace.

The self-centered servant didn't get it. The grace-given give grace.

A teen named Jacob Shepherd got it.

THE CHRISTMAS I GOT RICH

by Jacob Andrew Shepherd

When I was thirteen, my mom and I went shopping at a big Portland mall at Christmastime. My pockets were stuffed with cash. Some I'd earned, some was from relatives who thought I'd be better at picking out gifts than they were. I'd already bought gifts for my family. I couldn't wait to spend the whole wad on some cool clothes or maybe a video game.

My mom was as excited to be there as I was. She loves the holiday scents, music, and decorations you just don't find in our small town. Mostly, though, she loves people. She has a way of getting past the clothing or makeup and seeing the real person. On this trip to the mall, she saw Carla.

Carla was the type of girl that most people would look at out of the corner of their eye and then turn away from. She sat on a bench in old, worn-out clothes, black makeup, and no coat. She was a teenager, but the anger and pain on her face made her look much older.

Mom sat down right next to Carla. "Are you okay?"

"I'm fine," Carla mumbled without looking up.

Lots of times people answer like that, no matter how they feel. It didn't stop my mom. She lovingly persisted until Carla told her what was really wrong.

Tears began to stream down Carla's face as she poured out her past. She knew nothing about her real parents and had been in and out of foster homes all her life. When she turned eighteen, her last set of foster parents kicked her out because they no longer received government money to keep her. She lived under a bridge and ventured to the mall for warmth and discarded food scraps. Mom sensed there was more and kept asking questions. Carla burst into tears and told how she had given up her newborn baby for adoption the day before. She couldn't afford to marry her boyfriend, let alone care for a baby.

About this time a young man walked up. His clothes were tattered, and he was obviously not dressed for the Northwest winter. He shifted uncomfortably on his worn-out sneakers while Carla explained that Rich was also a foster kid who had been kicked out at age eighteen.

I couldn't imagine what it must feel like not to have parents who love and care for you. I never had to worry if I was going to have a next meal or clothes to wear. My biggest problem was keeping all my clothes off the floor in my room.

As I listened to Carla and Rich share their story through lonely tears, the pull that the mall had on me started to change. My heart sank, and my enthusiasm for more stuff sank with it.

What Mom and I did for the next two hours will always be burned in my memory. We went shopping, all right, but we went with two new friends. You should have seen the looks on Carla's and Rich's faces when Mom and I escorted them straight to Nordstrom Rack. They gasped. "We've never been in a store like this!"

Mom grabbed Carla's hand and headed straight for the women's section while Rich and I looked at men's clothing. "Those pants look great on you," I said as Rich stepped out of the dressing room. "Are you sure that jacket's going to be warm enough?"

After Rich and I picked out his jacket, pants, and shirt, we joined Mom and watched Carla model her clothes. Her faced beamed as we rooted her on. We headed for the cash register, and my mom dug into her purse. I quietly stopped her, patting my pocket of cash. "Mom, I have it this time."

So, what did I get for Christmas that year? I'd say I got Rich . . . a friend named Rich.[3]

In a big-city mall, grace happened. From God to a pair of Christmas shoppers to a couple of homeless teens. Generous, unexpected, overflowing grace.

What about you?

Do you resent God's kindness to others? Do you grumble at God's uneven compensation? If so, are you jealous because the Lord is good?

How long has it been since your generosity stunned someone? Since someone objected, "No, really, this is too generous"? If it's been a while, reconsider God's extravagant grace.

Let grace microwave your cold heart. "Grow in the grace and knowledge of our Lord and Savior Jesus Christ" (2 Peter 3:18). When you do, you'll find yourself joining the ranks of the truly wealthy. You'll be rich with grace.

6

WET FEET

Where grace is lacking, bitterness abounds.
Where grace abounds, forgiveness grows.

f hurts were hairs, we'd all look like grizzlies. Even the smooth-skinned beauty on the magazine cover, the sweet-singing star onstage, the kind old lady who lives next door. All of them. All of us. Furry, hairy beasts we'd become. If hurts were hairs, we'd be lost behind the thick of them.

After all, aren't there so many? So many hurts. When friends mock the way you dress, their insults hurt. When teachers ignore your work, their neglect hurts. When your mom embarrasses you, when your girlfriend snubs you, when your boyfriend drops you, it hurts. Rejection always does. As surely as summer brings sun, people bring pain. Sometimes deliberately. Sometimes randomly.

Victoria Ruvolo can tell you about random pain. On a November evening in 2004, this forty-four-year-old New Yorker was driving to her home on Long Island. She'd just attended her niece's recital and was ready for the couch, a warm fire, and relaxation.

She doesn't remember seeing the silver Nissan approach from the east. She remembers nothing of the eighteen-year-old leaning out the window, holding, of all things, a frozen turkey. He chucked it at her windshield.

The twenty-pound bird crashed through the glass, bent the steering wheel inward, and shattered her face like a dinner plate on concrete. The violent prank left her grappling for life in the intensive care unit. She survived, but only after doctors wired her jaw, affixed one eye by synthetic film, and bolted titanium plates to her skull. She can't look in the mirror without a reminder of her hurt.[1]

You weren't hit by a turkey, but you ride the bus with one, are on a class project with one, got dumped by one. Now where do you turn? Bud Light and friends? Pity Party Catering Service? Hitman.com?

When someone hurts us, we tend to want to return the "favor." That's just what some US soldiers in Afghanistan did. A troop member's girlfriend broke up with him by letter. He was devastated. To add insult to injury, his girl wrote, "Please return my favorite picture of myself because I would like to use that photograph for my engagement picture in the county newspaper."

> When someone hurts us, we tend to want to return the "favor."

Ouch! But his buddies came to his defense. They went throughout the barracks and collected pictures of all the other soldiers' girlfriends. They filled a shoebox. The jilted soldier mailed the photos to his ex-girlfriend with this note: "Please find your enclosed picture and return the rest. For the life of me I can't remember which one you were."[2]

Yes, retaliation has its appeal. But Jesus shows us a better path—a trail that ends in grace.

Jesus and his followers had gathered in an upstairs

chamber, the Upper Room, for Passover. He knew it was the final night before his death. What would he choose to do at this solemn and historic moment? "He got up from the table, took off his robe, wrapped a towel around his waist, and poured water into a basin. Then he began to wash the disciples' feet and to wipe them with the towel he had around him" (John 13:4–5 NLT).

> Jesus understood the who and why of his life.

Jesus understood the *who* and *why* of his life. Who was he? God's Son. Why was he on earth? To serve the Father. He knew his identity and authority. So Jesus—principal, head coach, king of the world, sovereign of the seas—washed feet.

I don't know about you, but if I knew I was about to die, my first thought wouldn't be to grab soap, water, and someone's ankle. I'm not even a fan of feet. Look you in the face? I will. Shake your hand? Gladly. Put an arm around your shoulders? Happy to do so. Rub a tear from the cheek of a child? In a heartbeat. But rub feet? Come on.

Feet stink. No one creates a cologne named Athlete's Foot Deluxe or Gym Sock Musk. Feet are not known for their sweet smell.

Nor their good looks. Your boyfriend doesn't tape a photo of your toes on his locker. Grandparents don't carry hoof pictures of their grandkids. "Aren't those the cutest arches you've ever seen?" We want to see the face, not the feet.

Did you hear about the man who was born with two left feet? He went out and bought some flip-flips.

Feet have heels. Feet have toenails. Bunions and fungus. Corns and calluses. And plantar warts! Some large enough to warrant a zip code. Feet have little piggies that go "Wee, wee, wee, all the way home."

Feet smell bad and look ugly. Which, I believe, is the point of this story.

Jesus touched the stinky, ugly FEET of his disciples. Knowing he came from God. Knowing he was going to God. Knowing he could arch an eyebrow or clear his throat, and every angel in the universe would snap to attention. Knowing that all authority was his, he exchanged his robe for the servant's wrap, lowered himself to knee level, and began to rub away the grime, grit, and grunge their feet had collected on the journey.

This was the assignment of the slave, the job of the servant. When a master came home from a day spent walking the cobblestone streets, he expected a foot washing. The lowliest servant met him at the door with towel and water.

But in the Upper Room there was no servant. Pitcher of water? Yes. Basin and towel? In the corner on the table. But no one touched them. No one stirred. Each disciple hoped someone else would reach for the basin and wash the feet.

Someone did.

Jesus didn't exclude a single follower, though we wouldn't have faulted him had he bypassed Philip. When Jesus told the disciples to feed a crowd of five thousand hungry people, Philip had retorted, "It's impossible!" (see John 6:7). So what does Jesus do with someone who questions his commands? Apparently, he washes the doubter's feet.

James and John pushed for front-row seats in Christ's kingdom (Mark 10:35–40). So what does Jesus do when people use his kingdom for personal advancement? He slides a basin in their direction.

Peter tried to talk Christ out of going to the cross (Matthew 16:21–22). Within hours Peter would deny even knowing Jesus and hightail his way into hiding (John 18:17, 25–27). In fact, all twenty-four of Jesus' followers' feet would soon scoot, leaving Jesus to face his accusers alone. Do you ever wonder what God does with promise breakers? He washes their feet.

And Judas. The lying, conniving, greedy rat who sold Jesus down the river for a pocket of cash. Jesus won't wash his feet, will he? Sure hope not. If he washes the feet of his Judas, you will have to wash the feet of yours. Your betrayer. Your turkey-throwing loser and lowlife. That ne'er-do-well, that good-for-nothing villain. Jesus' Judas walked away with thirty pieces of silver. Your Judas walked away with your reputation, idea, virginity, trust, best friend.

If grace were a wheat field, God's left you the state of Kansas.

You expect me to wash his feet and let him go?

Most people don't want to. They use the villain's photo as a dart target. Their internal volcano erupts every now and again, sending hate airborne, polluting and stinking the world. Most people keep a pot of anger on low boil.

But you aren't "most people." Grace has happened to you. Look at your feet. They are wet, grace soaked. Your toes and arches and heels have felt the cool basin of God's grace. Jesus has washed the grimiest parts of your life. He didn't bypass you and carry the basin toward someone else.

A pianist named Austin knew how to forgive. A mischievous kid named Kyle surely needed to be forgiven.

MUSIC LESSONS

by Katherine Bond

If anything went wrong at Orville Wright Elementary—fifteen pairs of underwear up the flagpole, a urinal that played "Jingle Bells" whenever someone flushed—whatever it was, Kyle got blamed.

I'm Kyle.

I'd been called, again, into Mrs. Kellerman's office. Sitting there was an older kid with skinny brown arms.

"Kyle, this is Austin Atterberry," Mrs. Kellerman said. She stuck a fat file—mine—back in the cabinet. "Austin is an eighth grader at Edison. He's agreed to be your Junior High Buddy."

So when did I agree to it? I thought.

The kid stood up. He was tall, real tall.

"I bet you play basketball," I said.

"Nope," he said, "piano."

It actually wasn't bad having Austin around. When I was with him, no one beat me up. He was right when he said he didn't play basketball. His shots always hit the rim. I beat him every time.

But he sure could play piano. He took lessons at a church from a lady named Mrs. Goodwin. He'd been making payments on a Yamaha PR-500 keyboard at Harmony Music. He told me he had a hundred dollars to go.

We went to the church for one of Austin's lessons. "Take Austin downstairs, Kyle," Mrs. Goodwin said. "There's something he should see."

Downstairs was a kitchen, some scratched tables, and a couple of high chairs. Then we saw it. Against the wall was Austin's Yamaha PR-500.

"Mrs. Goodwin!" Austin let out his breath. "How did you . . . ?"

Her bracelets jingled. "You've earned it, sugar."

Austin turned on the keyboard. He made it sound like a violin, he played drum rhythms, he made it sound like the school choir.

After a while, Austin and Mrs. Goodwin went upstairs for his lesson. I offered to babysit the keyboard. It was pretty cool. It could do trumpets and organ and something called vibraphone.

Then I got an idea. If I could make a urinal play "Jingle Bells," it would be easy to move a few wires and see if I could get a cow, a sheep, and a chicken. Austin would bust a gut laughing. I found a screwdriver and took off the back. I pulled the circuit board, messed with it, and reinstalled it. Then I pressed a key.

It sounded exactly like a strangled duck. So I pressed another key. Same thing. No bells, no drums. Just a shriek ending in a puttering wheeze.

Overhead the piano stopped. There were foot-steps on the stairs. I shoved wires back into the keyboard as fast as I could. Austin burst in and stopped. He looked at my fistful of wires. Without saying a word, he jammed a sourball in his mouth and left.

I found him on his knees in the sanctuary. Mrs. Goodwin was gone.

"What are you doing?" I asked.

"I'm praying that I don't kill you," he muttered through the sourball.

It was a good time to go back downstairs. I messed with more wires. Nothing worked. It wasn't my fault it had so many circuits. If Austin was going to be that way, there was no reason to stay.

There was a sour taste in my mouth as I rode the bus home.

Austin didn't show the next day. A week went by. I thought about all the basketball he'd played with me even though he always lost. Austin was a real friend.

And I wasn't.

Austin was playing the piano when I sneaked

into the sanctuary. His sad music seeped inside me. Two stupid tears dripped down my nose.

Austin looked up. I looked down and blinked my eyes a bunch of times. He walked up the aisle and put a hand on my shoulder. I didn't shake him off.

"I'm sorry," I mumbled, feeling the awkwardness of what I'd done. "I tried to fix it, but—"

Austin nodded.

"Are you . . . still mad?" How lame. He probably hated me.

"Jesus says to forgive," Austin said. "Forgive isn't a feeling, little bro. It's something you do."

"Will you still be my buddy?" I looked up at Austin, and he grinned.

"Yeah," he said. "I will, little bro. There are a few things you've still gotta learn."[3]

We also still have a few things to learn. One is that forgiveness is something you do. Another is how to accept unearned grace.

"Since I, the Lord and Teacher, have washed your feet, you ought to wash each other's feet. I have given you an example to follow. Do as I have done to you" (John 13:14–15 NLT).

To accept grace is to accept the promise to give it.

Nine months after Victoria Ruvolo's disastrous night, she stood titanium-bolted face-to-face with her offender in court. Ryan Cushing was no longer the cocky, turkey-tossing kid in the Nissan. He was trembling, tearful, and apologetic. For New York City he had come to symbolize a generation of kids out of control. People packed the room to see him get his punishment. The judge's sentence enraged them—only six months behind bars, five years' probation, some counseling, and public service.

The courtroom erupted. Everyone objected. Everyone, that is, except Victoria Ruvolo. She'd asked the judge for the light sentence. The boy walked over, and she embraced him. In full view of the judge and the crowd, she held him tight, stroked his hair. He sobbed, and she spoke: "I forgive you. I want your life to be the best it can be."[4]

She allowed grace to shape her response. "God gave me a second chance at life, and I passed it on," she says.[5] "If I hadn't let go of that anger, I'd be consumed by this need for revenge. Forgiving him helps me move on."[6]

To accept grace is to accept the promise to give it.

Her mishap led to her mission: volunteering with the county probation department. "I'm trying to help others, but I know for the rest of my life I'll be known as 'The Turkey Lady.' Could have been worse. He could have thrown a ham. I'd be Miss Piggy!"[7] Victoria Ruvolo knows how to fill a basin and wash someone's feet.

And you?

YOUR STORY:

When was the last time someone did something truly awful to you?

....

Did you respond with a grudge or with grace?

....

Build a prison of hate if you want, each brick a hurt. Design it with one cell and a single bunk. (You won't attract roommates.) Hang large video screens on each of the four walls so recorded images of the offense can play over and over, twenty-four hours a day. Headphones available on request. Appealing? No, appalling. Harbored grudges suck the joy out of life. Revenge won't paint the blue back in your sky or restore the spring in your step. No. It will leave you bitter, bent, and angry.

Instead, give the grace you've been given. You don't approve of the deeds of your offender when you do. Jesus didn't approve your sins by forgiving you. Grace doesn't tell you to pretend the bully didn't beat you up. It doesn't tell you to like the father who molested you. The grace-defined person still stands up against cheaters and liars and betrayers.

Grace is not blind. It sees the hurt full well. But grace chooses to see God's forgiveness even more. It refuses to let hurts poison the heart. Where grace is lacking, bitterness abounds. Where grace abounds, forgiveness grows.

Sequence matters. Jesus washes first; we wash next. He demonstrates; we follow. He uses the towel, then extends it to us, saying, "Now you do it. Walk across the floor of your Upper Room, and wash the feet of your Judas."

So go ahead. Get your feet wet. Remove your socks and shoes, and set your feet in the basin. First one, then the other. Let the hands of God wipe away every dirty part of your life—your dishonesty, jealousy, anger, bitterness, hypocrisy. Let him touch them all. As his hands do their work, look across the room. Someone is there with dirty feet, hoping you'll pick up the basin. Someone who needs grace.

> To be a Christian means to forgive the inexcusable, because God has forgiven the inexcusable in you.
>
> —C. S. Lewis

Forgiveness may not happen all at once. But it can happen with you. After all, you have wet feet.

7

FESSING UP

His grace has grabbed you, rewired you, and reserved your heavenly room. You can risk honesty with God.

liked beer.

Too much. Alcoholism haunts my family ancestry. I have early memories of following my father, Jack Lucado, through the halls of a rehab center to see his sister. I have more recent memories of watching my older brother, Dee, drink away health, relationships, jobs, money, and all but the last two years of his life. Beer doesn't mix well with my family DNA.

My father knew it. He hated drinking in every form because he understood its power to destroy. By the time I was fifteen, he'd left no doubt he wanted his kids to have nothing to do with alcohol. Funny thing about being fifteen, though. You just know you're smarter than your parents. At least about some things. At least, I decided, about drinking.

So I made a plan to get drunk. The details involved me, a friend, and a case of quarts. I drank beer until I couldn't see straight, then went home and vomited until I couldn't stand up. My dad came to the bathroom, smelled the beer, threw a towel in my direction, and walked away in disgust.

That was the beginning of some wayward years for one Max Lucado. I lied to my parents. I lied to friends. I focused on me, me, me.

And I drank. With gusto.

I was a sophomore in college the last time I got drunk. I'd quit going to church because I didn't think God would want me back. But the influence of a few good friends and a minister helped me see that the whole reason Jesus died on the cross was for people like me. It was a life-changing discovery. I realized that God is always ready to grant a second chance. So I grabbed it—and have been grateful ever since.

I also swore off drinking. For a while. Then one day I woke up to realize that after a few slipups and a lot of rationalizations, I had become the very thing I hate: a hypocrite. A pretender. Two-faced. Acting one way. Living another. It wasn't the beer but the cover-up that sickened me.

I knew what I needed to do.

"If we say we have no sin, we are fooling ourselves, and the truth is not in us. But if we confess our sins, he will forgive our sins, because we can trust God to do what is right. He will cleanse us from all the wrongs we have done" (1 John 1:8–9 NCV).

Confess. Admit. Come clean. Fess up. The words all mean the same thing—but what is that, exactly?

Confession isn't telling God what he doesn't know. Impossible.

Confession isn't complaining. If I just repeat my problems and woes, I'm whining.

Confession isn't blaming. Pointing fingers at others without pointing any at me feels good, but it doesn't bring healing.

Confession is so much more. Confession is a radical reliance on grace. A declaration of our trust in God's goodness. "What I did was bad," we admit, "but your grace is greater than my sin, so I confess it." If our understanding of grace is small, our confession will be small: reluctant, hesitant, incomplete, buried in excuses and qualifications. You know the kind. "Dad, uh, somehow the bumper on your car got scratched. Well, more than scratched. Maybe somebody

> Confession is a radical reliance on grace.

hit it while I was at the store?" Or "Hey, sis, sorry that I read your diary, but you really shouldn't have left it open on your bed."

Wild, overflowing grace, on the other hand, creates a full and honest confession. Like the one of the son who took his inheritance money, left home, blew it all, and returned in shame to say, "Father, I have sinned against heaven and in your sight, and am no longer worthy to be called your son" (Luke 15:21).

Or like the one offered by Shaun Groves.

A BILLION LIGHT-YEARS FROM GOD

by Shaun Groves

I was thirteen. I was at my friend Tyler's house. Tyler was my only friend with Internet access.

Almost every day, we played computer games for hours.

But one day we clicked on what we thought was a game to download, and our lives changed. It wasn't a game, but a video. At first, we laughed when we saw the blurry, slow-moving image of a woman. We laughed nervously as if to say, "That's so stupid. Turn it off." But we didn't turn it off. We watched it. Then I went home.

But Tyler kept looking for more and showed me what he found. I didn't run away this time. I didn't want to keep looking. But I did. I was caught.

As time went on, I bounced between feeling guilty and wanting to see more. Some days I was strong. Other days I was like a lustful porn addict looking for a fix. I searched my friends' houses in hopes their dad had a hidden stash of *Playboy* somewhere. When that didn't work, I stole porn magazines from convenience store shelves.

But the pleasure from those pictures always faded. And in its wake I fought pounding waves of regret and guilt. I felt a million miles from good, a billion light-years from God. I knew I was a Christian. And I knew God saw me as perfect and lovable as he saw his very own Son. I knew all this. Grace. Love. Forgiveness.

But I didn't feel it. And I grew more and more depressed and frustrated with myself. I promised myself over and over that I wouldn't mess up again, only to repeat my mistakes.

Finally, I couldn't take it anymore. I got help. I was hanging out with a close friend who was a strong believer. Out of nowhere, I told him everything. My voice shaking, I confessed that if I could look at pornography for free, knowing I wouldn't be found out or feel guilty, I would. I asked him for help. We prayed together.

And then—to my surprise—my friend told me he had the same problem. We went to an older Christian in our church and asked him to help us. He listened, gave us wise advice, and prayed. The first thing he showed us was that we weren't the only ones with these problems. We weren't freaks.

As an adult, I've learned to limit my opportunities for temptation. I don't walk alone into the magazine section of a store. I don't have some catalogs in my house. I don't watch TV alone. I have Internet filters. Even with filters, I don't go online if no one else is home.

I also read the Bible and write down what I've learned or what I think I'll do differently because of it. I spend time in silence asking God to speak to me.

And I have honest relationships with Christian guys. I have one friend in particular I check in with daily. We talk about sex and sin and the junk that tempts us. We gripe. We teach. We confess. And we pray: "God, help me do what's right today. And help Tyler too. Save us both from pornography, and make us closer to perfect."[1]

Confession was good for Shaun Groves. It was also good for King David, even though he took a mighty long time to get to it. This Old Testament hero dedicated a season of his life to making stupid, idiotic, godless decisions.

Stupid decision #1: David didn't go to war with his soldiers. He stayed home with too much time on his hands and, apparently, romance on his mind. While walking on his balcony, he spotted the beautiful Bathsheba, bathing.

Stupid decision #2: David sent servants to bring Bathsheba to his palace and escort her into his bedroom, where rose petals carpeted the floor and champagne chilled in the corner. A few weeks later she told him that she was expecting his child.

Stupid decisions #3, 4, and 5: David tricked Bathsheba's husband, murdered him, and behaved as if he'd done nothing wrong. The baby was born, and David still pretended that everything was fine.

Yet he knew it wasn't. Anything but. So he finally talked to God about it. "O LORD, don't rebuke me in your anger! Don't discipline me in your rage! Your arrows have struck deep, and your blows are crushing me. Because of your anger, my whole body is sick; my health is broken because of my sins. . . . My wounds fester and stink because of my foolish sins. I am bent over and racked with pain" (Psalm 38:1–3, 5–6 NLT).

Bury misbehavior and expect pain, period. Unconfessed sin is a knife blade lodged in the soul. You cannot escape the misery it creates.

Ask Li Fuyan. This Chinese man tried every treatment imaginable to ease his throbbing headaches. Nothing helped. An X-ray finally revealed the culprit. A rusty four-inch knife blade had been lodged in his skull for four years. In an attack by a robber, Fuyan had suffered lacerations on the right side of his jaw. He didn't know the blade had broken off inside his head.[2]

> Unconfessed sin is a knife blade lodged in the soul.

No wonder he suffered from such stabbing pain! (Sorry. Couldn't resist.)

We can't live with foreign objects buried in our bodies. Or our souls. What would an X-ray of your insides show? Regret over the rude way you ended a relationship? Remorse over losing your temper? Shame about the habit you couldn't quit, the temptation you didn't resist, or the courage you couldn't find? Guilt lies hidden beneath the surface, annoying, gnawing. Sometimes so deeply embedded you don't know the cause.

You become moody, cranky. You tend to overreact. You're angry, irritable. You can be touchy, you know. Understandable, since you have a blade of shame lodged in your soul.

YOUR STORY:

When was the last time you tried to hide something you were ashamed of?

....

How did that turn out for you?

....

Maybe it's time to remove the problem. How? Fess up. Request a spiritual X-ray. As God brings misbehavior to mind, agree with him and apologize. Let him apply grace to the wounds.

That's what David did. After a year of denial and a cover-up, he finally prayed, "God, be merciful to me because you are loving. Because you are always ready to be merciful, wipe out all my wrongs. Wash away all my guilt and make me clean again" (Psalm 51:1–2 NCV).

David waved the white flag. No more combat. No more arguing with heaven. He came clean with God. And you? Your moment might look something like this.

Late evening. Bedtime. The pillow beckons. But so does your guilty conscience. An encounter with a friend turned nasty earlier in the day. Words were exchanged. Accusations made. Lines drawn in the sand. Names called. Rude, crude behavior. You bear some, if not most, of the blame.

The old version of you would try to pretend it never happened. Too late now, right?

But you aren't the old version of you. Grace is happening, rising like a morning sun over a wintry meadow, scattering shadows, melting frost. Warmth. God doesn't scowl at the sight of you. You once thought he did. Arms crossed and angry, perpetually ticked off. Now you know better. Out of love, his grace has grabbed you, rewired you, and reserved your heavenly room. You can risk honesty with God.

> But you aren't the old version of you. Grace is happening.

You tell the pillow to wait, and you step into the presence of Jesus. "Can we talk about today's argument? I am sorry that I reacted in the way I did. I was harsh, judgmental, and impatient. You have given me so much grace. I gave so little. Please forgive me."

There—doesn't that feel better? No hall pass or perfect speech required. Just a prayer. The prayer will likely prompt an apology, and the apology will quite possibly preserve a friendship and protect a heart. You might even hang a sign on your bedroom wall: "Grace happens here."

Or maybe your prayer needs to probe deeper. Beneath the outer layer of today's deeds are unresolved actions of the past. Like King David, you made one stupid decision after another. You stayed when you should have gone, looked when you should have turned, flirted when you should have walked away, hurt when you should have helped, denied when you should have confessed.

> The confession of evil works is the first beginning of good works.
>
> —Augustine

Talk to God about these buried blades. Go to him as you would go to a trusted family member. Explain the pain, and revisit your mistake together. Welcome his healing touch. And—this is important—trust his ability to receive your confession more than your ability to make it. The power of confession lies not with the person who makes it but with the God who hears it.

When you do this, God may send you to talk to another Christian. "Confess your sins to *one another*, and pray for one another so that you may be healed" (James 5:16 NASB, emphasis mine). James calls us not only to confess *up* to God but also to confess *out* to each other.

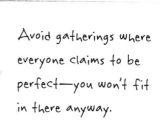

Avoid gatherings where everyone claims to be perfect—you won't fit in there anyway.

People are attracted to honesty. You should be too. So find a Bible study or youth group with guys and gals who believe in fessing up. Avoid gatherings where everyone claims to be perfect—you won't fit in there anyway. Instead, hang out where people admit their sins and show humility. Healing happens in places like this.

Confessors find a freedom that deniers don't.

"If we say we have no sin, we are fooling ourselves, and the truth is not in us. But if we confess our sins, he will forgive our sins, because we can trust God to do what is right. He will cleanse us from all the wrongs we have done" (1 John 1:8–9 NCV).

Oh, the sweet certainty of these words. "He *will* cleanse us." Not he *might, could, would,* or *has been known to.* He *will* cleanse you. Tell God what you did. Again, not that he doesn't already know, but the two of you need to agree. Spend as much time as you need. Share all the details you can. Then let the pure water of grace flow over your mistakes.

BETTER THAN PERFECT

Our merits merit nothing. God's work merits everything.

S even minutes. That's all the time left for you to finish writing your speech, comb your hair, and slip onstage. The auditorium is filled with fellow students for the Veteran's Day assembly. It's your job to introduce the speakers and put some perspective on the event. Perspective? Who has perspective at a moment like this? You're so stressed your hands are shaking. Why did you sign up for this? Why didn't you write your speech last night?

You know why. To get an A in leadership class, you needed more activity credits. And to get As in math and English, you had to finish those extra credit projects last night. Even if it meant staying up until 2 a.m. Again.

Is the pressure getting to you? Maybe. There's so much of it. Pressure from parents to get top grades to get scholarships to get into the best college. Pressure at your part-time job at the Snow Cone to show up earlier, serve faster, smile bigger. Pressure from the band teacher to keep those rowdy sophomore sax players in line. Pressure from one group of friends to say and wear the right thing. Pressure from another group to work less and hang out more. Pressure from your Christian friends to go to youth group and stay up on your Bible reading.

And then there's the pressure you put on yourself. You've always been the model child, the standout student. You *want* to be the best. Sure, it's tough keeping everyone happy. But it's all part of the plan. You just need to be perfect.

That's what God expects, right?

The Pharisees seemed to think so. During Jesus' time on earth, the spiritual leaders of the day focused on observing the rules of religion. They prayed when it was time to pray. Worshiped when it was time to worship. Rested when it was time to rest. They went out of their way to impress God with their dutifulness and dedication to directions. They strove to be perfect in God's eyes—and preferred that everyone around them be perfect too.

Maybe that's why they got so upset with the stranger from Galilee. This Jesus didn't follow the rules. He healed when he was supposed to rest. Taught when he was supposed to listen. Dined with people he was supposed to shun.

And he introduced an idea that made no sense to them: grace. He talked about a ticket to heaven that wasn't punched by good deeds but by repentance and faith. "For God so loved the world that he gave his one and only Son, that whoever believes in him shall not perish but have eternal life" (John 3:16 NIV).

A few years later, a Roman jailer was put in charge of a pair of prisoners named Paul and Silas. He was told to guard them carefully, so he marched them into an inner cell and fastened their feet in chains. Only they didn't stay fastened. God had a different plan.

That night an earthquake awakened the drowsy jailer. It also released every door and chain in the prison. The jailer knew an act of God when he saw one. Trembling in awe and fear, he fell before Paul and Silas and asked, "Sirs, what must I do to be saved?" (Acts 16:30).

What must I do? The question echoes through the centuries. In the deepest cavern of our hearts, we understand that we don't deserve heaven. We don't measure up to the Almighty. We're broken pieces of sand dollars in an ocean of treasure—a long way from perfect. So we have a hard time with this thing called grace.

"What must I do?" The question echoes through the centuries.

It's not that we don't believe in grace. We do. We believe in grace a lot. We just don't believe in grace alone. Surely, we think, it takes more than grace to save us. We grace-a-lots want to do our part. We figure Jesus *almost* finished the work of our salvation but every so often needs our help. So we give it.

YOUR STORY:

Do you believe in grace alone?

....

Do you ever try to add your work to God's grace? How?

....

We collect good works the way Boy Scouts collect merit badges on a sash. I kept mine on a hook in my closet, not to hide it, but so I could see it. No morning was complete without a satisfying glance at this exhibit of excellence. If you've ever owned a Boy Scout merit-badge sash, you understand the affection I felt.

Each oval emblem rewarded my hard work. I paddled across a lake to earn the canoe badge, swam laps to earn the swimming badge, and carved a totem pole to earn the woodworking badge. Could anything be more gratifying than earning merit badges?

Yes. Showing them off. Which I did every Thursday when Boy Scouts wore uniforms to middle school. I strode through the campus as if I were the king of England.

The merit-badge system tidies life. Achievements result in compensation. Accomplishments receive applause. Guys envied me. Girls swooned. My female classmates managed to keep their hands to themselves only by virtue of extreme self-control. I knew they secretly longed to run a finger over my signaling badge and to ask me to spell their names in Morse code.

I became a Christian about the same time I became a Boy Scout and made the assumption that God grades on a merit system too. Good Scouts move up. Good people go to heaven. Perfect people get the best seats.

So I resolved to amass a multitude of spiritual badges. An embroidered Bible for Bible reading. Folded hands for prayer. A kid sleeping on a pew for church attendance. In my imagination, angels feverishly stitched emblems on my behalf. They scarcely kept pace with my performance and wondered if one sash would suffice. "That Lucado kid is exhausting my fingers!" I worked toward the day, the great day, when God, amid falling confetti and celebratory shouts, would drape my badge-laden sash across my chest and welcome me into his eternal kingdom, where I could humbly display my badges for eternity.

But some thorny questions came up. If God saves good people, how good is "good"? God expects us to have integrity of speech, but how much? What is the permitted percentage of exaggeration? Suppose the required score is 80 and I score a 79? How do you know your score?

I asked a minister about it. Surely he would help me answer the "How good is 'good'?" question. He did, with one word: *do.* Do better. Do more. Do now. Do. Do. Do.

> If God saves good people, how good is "good"?

You've probably heard a version of this from your parents, your teachers, your friends, maybe even your pastor. Do good, and you'll be okay. Do more, and you'll be saved. Keep doing until you get it right.

Keep doing until you're perfect.

Most people embrace the idea that God saves good people. So be good! Be moral. Be honest. Be kind. Keep your promises. Pray five times a day. Be on time. Do your homework. Earn merit badges.

That was Carla Barnhill's approach to life—until she figured out a better way.

IF ONLY I COULD BE PERFECT

by Carla Barnhill

It happened when I was twelve, but I remember the moment like it happened this morning. My older brother had gotten himself into trouble—again. My mom and I were folding laundry, talking about the situation and how worried she was about my brother's actions. Then she said to me, "I know we'll never have to worry about you, honey."

Now, my mom meant it as a compliment. Her intention was to tell me she knew I was well-behaved and smart enough to avoid some of the stuff that had gotten my brother in hot water. But in my mind, her words set a huge weight on my shoulders. When she said, "We'll never have to worry about you," I heard, "Make *sure* we never have to worry about you."

That simple conversation set me on a mission—to be the perfect daughter. My goal was to make sure my parents never had a doubt about where I was, what I was doing, or who I was with. So I never missed a curfew, never drank a beer, never hung out with anyone who might lead me into trouble.

Those few times I *did* get into trouble with my parents, I felt horrible. And even though I got off with a few stern words, I still felt like I'd let them down.

My desire to be perfect carried over to my relationship with God. I honestly thought God would love me more if I went to youth group, if I said my prayers, if I went to Bible camp. I believed I could impress God if I did all the right Christian things. I didn't always do those things because I wanted to. I did them because I wanted God to think I was perfect.

Striving for excellence isn't always a bad thing. Doing our best is part of the Christian life. Way back in the Old Testament, God's people were told to "present as the Lord's portion the best and holiest part of everything given to you" (Numbers 18:29 NIV). Even though God was talking about tithes and offerings, we know our *whole lives* are offerings to God, and that we need to give God our best.

But perfectionism is "doing our best" for all the wrong reasons. Perfectionism is about us, not about God.

I was being good because I thought it would help me earn love and acceptance. If my behavior pleased my parents, they'd love me even more. If my behavior pleased God, I'd earn his favor. I came to believe my worth was based on how good I was—and on how good other people thought I was.

Inside, I was stressed-out. The pressure to

be perfect was almost too much to handle. But I didn't think I could tell anyone how I felt because that would mean admitting I wasn't perfect. And that was the last thing I wanted to do.

I know I'm not the only one who has felt like being a good person—being a perfect Christian—is the key to God's heart. One of my friends once told me she didn't think she was good enough to be a Christian. She didn't think she could live up to the expectations everyone had of Christians—always being nice, never getting into trouble. She saw Christianity as a secret club that only the "good" kids could belong to. My efforts to be the perfect person sure didn't help her think otherwise. But if I'd have been more honest about my own failures and shown her how God forgives, she might have felt differently.

Perfectionism is a losing game. Fortunately, it's one we really don't have to play. After all, God reached out to us when we were as far away from him as we could possibly be. Being a Christian isn't about being perfect; it's about being forgiven. So we can relax and be confident that God knows we're not perfect and loves us just the same.[1]

There's a problem with pushing for perfection. Trying to be good still doesn't answer the fundamental question: what level of good is good enough? At stake is our eternal destination, yet we are more confident about cookie recipes and baseball stats than the entrance requirements for heaven.

> What level of good is good enough?

God has a better idea: "For by grace you have been saved through faith, and that not of yourselves; it is the gift of God" (Ephesians 2:8). We contribute nothing. Zilch. As opposed to the merit badge of the Scout, salvation of the soul is unearned. A gift. Our merits merit nothing. God's work merits everything.

You've seen in the last few chapters how to activate God's grace. Give. Forgive. Confess. Trust. But salvation is the one where you don't *do* grace. Instead, do nothing. Believe and let it happen to you. When you allow God to move in, he does the doing. When his grace gets inside you, it's a new start on life. You could call it a spiritual heart transplant.

Tara Storch understands this miracle as much as anyone might. Her daughter, Taylor, was a popular and busy eighth grader. Taylor played volleyball and was in the band. She took the toughest classes. She made silly YouTube videos with her brother. But in the spring of 2010, a skiing accident took Taylor's life.

What followed was every family's worst nightmare: a funeral, a burial, a flood of questions and tears. Her parents decided to donate Taylor's organs to needy patients. Few people needed a heart more than Patricia Winters. Her heart had begun to fail five years earlier, leaving her too weak to do much more than sleep. Taylor's heart gave Patricia a future again.

Taylor's mom had only one request: she wanted to hear the heart of her daughter. She and her husband, Todd, flew from Dallas to Phoenix and went to Patricia's home. The two women embraced for a long time, soon to be joined by Todd. After a few moments, Tara took a stethoscope, placed it against Patricia's chest, and heard Taylor's heartbeat again.

"It's so strong," the mother whispered.

"*She* is very strong," Patricia assured.

Mom and Dad took turns listening. They heard the still-beating heart of their daughter, even though it indwelled a different body.[2] When God hears your heart, he hears the still-beating heart of his Son. As Paul said, "It is no longer I who live, but Christ lives in me" (Galatians 2:20). The apostle sensed within himself not just the philosophy, ideals, or influence of Christ but the person of Jesus. Christ moved in. He still does. When grace happens, Christ enters. "Christ in you, the hope of glory" (Colossians 1:27).

No other religion or philosophy makes such a claim. No other movement implies the living presence of its founder *in* his followers. Mohammed does not indwell Muslims. Buddha does not inhabit Hindus. Lady Gaga does not reside in even her most fervent fans. Influence? Instruct? Entice? Yes. But occupy? No.

Yet Christians embrace this puzzling promise. "The mystery in a nutshell is this: Christ is in you" (Colossians 1:27 MSG). The Christian is a person in whom Christ is happening. He moves in, making himself at home. We sense his rearranging. Confusion turns into clear direction. Bad choices are replaced by better ones. Little by little a new self emerges. "He decided from the outset to shape the lives of those who love him along the same lines as the life of his Son" (Romans 8:29 MSG).

Grace is God as heart surgeon cracking open your chest, removing your heart, poisoned as it is with pride and pain, and replacing it with his own. His dream isn't just to get you into heaven, but heaven into you.

That's exactly what happened to Patricia Winters. She got a little bit of heaven in the form of a young girl's heart. For Patricia, it was a gift of new life. A gift she did nothing to merit. A gift that meant everything.

A gift of grace.

The same gift confronted the earthquake-shaken Roman jailer. Remember? He asked, "What must I do to be saved?" Paul's answer to the jailer and to every grace-a-lot has nothing to do with doing: "Believe in the Lord Jesus, and you will be saved" (Acts 16:31 NIV).

Short. Simple. Yet more profound than the most scholarly textbook.

All our striving, struggling, sweating, and suffering won't swing open the door to salvation. All our good deeds won't grease the gates of heaven. Frankly, I get tired of being tired, of trying to perform my way into a picture of the perfect Christian. I'd rather give up and accept the gift of grace.

How about you?

Maybe we need to follow the example of the Chilean miners. Trapped beneath two thousand feet of solid rock, the thirty-three men were desperate. The collapse of a main tunnel had sealed their exit and thrust them into survival mode. They ate two spoonfuls of tuna, a sip of milk, and a morsel of peaches—every other day. For two months they prayed for someone to save them.

On the surface above, the Chilean rescue team worked around the clock, consulting NASA, meeting with experts. They designed a thirteen-foot-tall capsule and drilled, first a communication hole, then an excavation tunnel. There was no guarantee of success. No one had ever been trapped underground this long and lived to tell about it.

Now someone has.

On October 13, 2010, the men began to emerge, slapping high fives and leading victory chants. A great-grandfather. A forty-four-year-old who was planning a wedding. Then a nineteen-year-old. All had different stories, but all had made the same decision. They trusted someone else to save them. No one returned the rescue offer with a declaration of independence: "I can get out of here on my own. Just give me a new drill." They had stared at the stone tomb long enough to reach the unanimous opinion: "We need help. We need someone to penetrate this world and pull us out." And when the rescue capsule came, they climbed in.

Why is it so hard for us to do the same?

We find it easier to trust the miracle of resurrection than the miracle of grace. We so fear failure that we create the image of perfection, lest heaven be even more disappointed in us than we are. The result? The most burned-out people on earth.

Attempts at self-salvation guarantee nothing but

> Faith's only function is to receive what grace offers.
>
> —John Stott

exhaustion. We scamper and scurry, trying to please God, collecting merit badges and brownie points and scowling at anyone who questions our accomplishments. Call us the church of hound-dog faces and slumped shoulders.

Enough. Enough of this frantic push to be perfect. "Your hearts should be strengthened by God's grace, not by obeying rules" (Hebrews 13:9 NCV). Jesus does not say, "Come to me, all you who are perfect and sinless." Just the opposite. "Come to Me, all who are weary and heavy-laden, and I will give you rest" (Matthew 11:28 NASB).

> Attempts at self-salvation guarantee nothing but exhaustion.

There is no fine print. It's not a magician's trick. God's promise has no hidden language. Let grace happen, for heaven's sake. No more pressure. No more performing. Of all the things you must earn in life, God's unending affection is not one of them. You have it.

If you ask me, that sounds perfect.

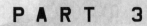

PART 3

THE
ROAD
HOME

9

YOU BELONG

"I, God, have made my choice. I choose you to be part of my forever family."

magine that you're dirty, tired, and hungry. You've ridden a tightly packed train for the last three days. You're surrounded by people but don't know any of them. Your parents are dead, and your brother and sister missing. You've got no possessions, no connections, no family, no future.

You're alone in the world.

Now you and a crowd of kids equally dirty and scared are lined up on a dusty platform like livestock at an auction. A group of locals, farmers by the look of them, eye you up and down. One steps in your direction. With callused fingers, he pulls down your lip and mutters, "Teeth're all right." Then he jabs your belly. "Nah, too skinny. Maybe the next one."

Welcome to life on the Orphan Train.

Between 1854 and 1929, about two hundred thousand orphans and abandoned children in Eastern cities were placed on westbound trains and shipped across the United States in search of homes and families. Many of the children had lost their parents in epidemics. Others were children of down-on-their-luck immigrants. Some were orphaned by the Civil War, others by alcohol.

But they all needed homes. Loaded on trains in groups of thirty to forty, they stopped in rural areas for viewings. Potential parents asked questions, poked, and prodded. If selected, the children went to their homes. If not, they got back on the train.

Lee Nailling remembers the experience. He'd been living at the Jefferson County Orphan Home for two years when he, as an eight-year-old, was taken with his two younger brothers to a train station in New York City. The day before, his biological father had handed Lee a pink envelope that bore his dad's name and address. He told the boy to write him as soon as he reached his destination. The boy placed the envelope within his coat pocket so no one would take it. The train embarked for Texas. Lee and his brothers fell asleep. When he awoke, the pink envelope was gone. He never saw it again.

What I'd love to tell you is that Lee's father found him. That the man, unwilling to pass another second without his sons, sold every possession so he could reunite his family. I'd love to describe the moment when Lee heard his father say, "Son, it's me! I came for you." Lee Nailling's biography, however, contains no such event.

But yours does.

Long before [God] laid down earth's foundations, he had us in mind, had settled on us as the focus of his love, to be made whole and holy by his love. Long, long

ago he decided to adopt us into his family through
Jesus Christ. (What pleasure he took in planning this!)
(Ephesians 1:4–5 MSG)

There is something in you that God loves. Not just
appreciates or approves but loves. You cause his eyes to
widen, his heart to beat faster. He loves you. Accepts you.
Desperately wants you in his family.

Don't we all yearn to be loved and accepted? To belong?
A boy named Brian did.

Brian was a special-education student at a small
high school. Most of his classmates teased and
laughed at him until another student, Mike, told
them to knock it off. From that moment, Mike
had a new buddy.

Later that week, Mike invited Brian to his house
to play video games. Brian kept asking questions
about God and why Mike was different from the
other kids. Mike explained that God loved Brian
the way he was, that he'd sent Jesus to earth to
die on the cross, rise from the dead, and make it
possible for everyone to spend eternity in heaven
if they believed. Mike showed Brian verses in the
Bible about God's love. Mike didn't know if Brian

understood everything he said, but when he fin-
ished Brian was ready to pray. With Mike's help,
Brian confessed that he was a sinner and invited
God into his heart.

"Brian," Mike said, "if you meant those words
you just prayed, where is Jesus right now?"

Brian pointed to his heart. "He's in here now."

Then Brian did something Mike would never forget. He hugged the Bible to his chest, lay down,
and let the tears flow down the side of his cheeks.
What Mike didn't know was that Brian's dad had left
the family when Brian was five years old. As Brian
had stood on the porch that day, his dad had told
him he was leaving because he couldn't deal with
having a son like him anymore. Then he had walked
out of Brian's life and was never seen again.

Brian had been looking for a father's love ever
since. He just wanted to be accepted. To belong.

That day at his new friend's house, Brian
found what he was looking for.[1]

So many messages tell us we don't belong. We get cut
from the basketball team. Dropped from the honor roll. Left
off the sleepover list. Everything from acne to Alzheimer's
leaves us feeling like the kid with no date to the prom.

We react. We validate our existence with a flurry of activity. We do more, buy more, achieve more. We try to say the right things, get the right look, hang with the right people. We try to fit in. All of it is a way of asking the burning question in our hearts: "Do I belong?"

God has an answer. His grace—outrageous, overflowing, stretching beyond the stars and back again—is the definitive reply. "Be blessed, my child. I love you. I accept you. I have adopted you into my family."

Adopted children are chosen children.

That's not the case with biological children. When the doctor handed Max Lucado to Jack Lucado, my dad had no exit option. No loophole. No choice. He couldn't give me back to the doctor and ask for a better-looking or smarter son. The hospital made him take me home.

But if you were adopted, your parents chose you. Surprise pregnancies happen. But surprise adoptions? Never heard of one. Your parents could have picked a different gender, color, or ancestry. But they selected you.

> God is love. He didn't need us. But he wanted us. And that is the most amazing thing.
>
> —Rick Warren

They wanted you in their family.

You object. "Oh, but if they could have seen the rest of my life, they might have changed their minds." My point exactly.

God saw your entire life from beginning to end, birth to hearse, and in spite of what he saw, he still dreams of having you by his side. Even with your faults and failures. Despite your muddles and missteps. He still stands near, arms open wide, ready to embrace you with a Father's love.

Annie, a high school senior, has an idea what that can be like.

OUTSTRETCHED ARMS

by LaDonna Gatlin

The morning started off in the usual way. Our daughter, Annie, pulled away from the curb of our home in her little black Mustang and headed off to school just like she had every other morning of that fall semester. She was a senior at our suburban Dallas high school and would be in the first graduating class of the new century. Annie was really enjoying her senior year and looking forward to going to college, where she planned to become a second-grade schoolteacher.

At 9:30 a.m., I was having my second cup of coffee and checking my e-mail in my home office. The home phone rang. The school nurse said, "Annie is here in my office, and she has something she needs to tell you." Well, a huge lump jumped up in my throat as my daughter got on the phone. Between her sobs I could barely make out what she was saying, but there was no mistake about what I heard next: "Mom, I'm pregnant."

I stifled a sob of my own and said, "Come home, honey, just come home." I immediately called my husband, Tim, on his cell phone. He was en route to the church where he is pastor of worship and administration. Through tears I told him the news, and he headed back home.

A few minutes later I heard the garage door open, signaling Tim's arrival. I looked out the living room window, and that little black Mustang was pulling up to the front curb. Tim rushed in from the garage door and opened the front door just in time for Annie to run up the steps and into her father's outstretched arms. I stood there in tearful amazement, watching the two of them in a silent embrace that truly said it all: "I love you. I forgive you. I'm here for you."

Our daughter graduated with her class on May 19, and gave birth to our first grandchild, an eight-and-a-half-pound boy, on July 12. Within minutes after he was born, she handed him to her daddy, who extended his arms for him. As we caressed this new life, we knew, without a doubt, that our greatest blessings may come through circumstances we never dreamed we'd experience. It's up to us to love unconditionally and be ready with outstretched arms.[2]

We all have a Father who loves us like this. We can live "like God's very own children, adopted into his family—calling him 'Father, dear Father.' . . . And since we are his children, we will share his treasures—for everything God gives to his Son, Christ, is ours, too" (Romans 8:15, 17 NLT).

It really is this simple. To accept God's grace is to accept God's offer to be adopted into his family.

> To accept God's grace is to accept God's offer to be adopted into his family.

Your identity is not in your friends, possessions, talents, tattoos, grades, or accomplishments. Nor are you defined by your family's divorce or debt, or your dumb choices. You are God's child. You get to call him "Papa." You "may approach God with freedom and confidence" (Ephesians 3:12 NIV). You receive the blessings of his special love (1 John 4:9–11) and provision (Luke 11:11–13). And you will inherit the riches of Christ and reign with him forever (Romans 8:17).

The adoption is horizontal as well as vertical. You are included in the forever family. Dividing walls of hostility are broken down, and community is created on the basis of a common father. Instant family worldwide!

Rather than try to invent reasons to feel good about yourself, trust God's verdict. If God loves you, you must be worth loving. If he wants to have you in his kingdom, then you must be worth having. God's grace invites you—no, *requires* you—to change your attitude about yourself and take sides with God against your feelings of rejection.

God loves each of us as if there were only one of us.

—Augustine

YOUR STORY:

On a scale of 1 to 10, with 10 being "I belong completely," how much do you feel you belong in your family?

....

How about in God's family?

....

Many years ago I traveled to my mother's house in west Texas to see my uncle. He had journeyed from California to visit the grave of my dad. He hadn't been able to make it to the funeral some months earlier.

Uncle Billy reminded me of my father. They looked so much alike: square bodied and ruddy complexion. We laughed, talked, and reminisced. When time came for me to leave, Uncle Billy followed me out to my car. We paused to say good-bye. He reached up and placed his hand on my shoulder and said, "Max, I want you to know, your dad was very proud of you."

I contained the emotion until I pulled away. Then I began to blubber like a six-year-old.

We never outgrow our need for a father's love. We were wired to receive it. May I serve the role of an Uncle Billy in your life? The hand on your shoulder is mine. The words I give you are God's. Receive them slowly. Don't filter, resist, downplay, or deflect them. Just receive them.

> We never outgrow our need for a father's love.

My child, I want you in my new kingdom. I have swept away your offenses like the morning clouds, your sins like the morning mist. I have redeemed you. The transaction is sealed; the matter is settled. I, God, have made my choice. I choose you to be part of my forever family.

Let these words cement in your heart a deep, satisfying, fear-quenching confidence that God will never let you go. You belong to him.

Lee Nailling experienced such security. Remember the eight-year-old orphan who lost his father's letter? Things got worse before they got better. He and his two brothers were taken to several towns. On the sixth day, someone in a small Texas town adopted one brother. Then a family selected Lee and his other brother. But soon Lee was sent to another home, the home of a farming family. He'd never been on a farm. The city boy didn't know not to open the doors of the chicks' cages. When Lee did, the angry farmer sent him away.

In a succession of sad events, Lee had lost his father, had ridden a train from New York to Texas, had been separated from his two brothers, and had been kicked out of two homes. His little heart was about to break. Finally he was taken to the home of a tall man and a short, plump woman. During the first supper Lee said nothing. He went to bed making plans to run away. The next morning they seated him at a breakfast of biscuits and gravy. He reached for one . . . until Mrs. Nailling stopped him. What had he done wrong this time?

"First we say grace," Mrs. Nailling said. She bowed her head. So did Mr. Nailling. Then, in a quiet voice, Mrs. Nailling thanked "our Father" for the breakfast, for the new day, and "for the privilege of raising a son."

Lee wasn't sure he'd heard right. A privilege? Him? He stared at the woman across the table. She smiled back. Even Mr. Nailling began to grin. Lee wasn't in trouble after all. Something strange was happening.

Lee had heard of the "our Father" Mrs. Nailling spoke of. When preachers came to the orphanage, they talked about an "our Father who art in heaven." But the Naillings talked as if this Father were right in the room with them. Lee noticed the empty chair next to him and wondered. Maybe, somehow, he was there.

"Help us make right choices as we guide him," Mrs. Nailling prayed, "and help him make right choices too." Lee realized she was talking about him. He was so busy thinking about all this that he barely heard Mr. Nailling say, "Dig in, son." Lee piled biscuits on his plate and considered his choices. Hate. Anger. Running away. Was it possible there was another option?

Later that morning, the Naillings and Lee went for a walk. The plan was to get Lee a haircut at the barbershop, but the Naillings were apparently in no hurry since they visited each of the six homes along the way. At the first stop, the Naillings introduced Lee as "our new son." It happened again at the second house. And the third. At each one, in fact.

By the time Lee and the Naillings finally reached the barbershop, he knew what choice he'd make. He wouldn't be running away. He'd found a home . . . and maybe something even better. Though he'd lost one father, it seemed he now had two more. Two fathers who might just love him.

Lee had a feeling he belonged to them both.[3]

To live as God's child is to know, at this very instant, that you are loved by your Maker, not because you try to please him and succeed or fail to please him and apologize, but because he wants to be your Father. Nothing more. All your efforts to win his affection are unnecessary. All your fears of losing his affection are needless. You can no more make him want you than you can convince him to abandon you.

The adoption is irreversible. You belong at his table.

10

SAVED FOR SURE

Trust God's hold on you more than your hold on God.

Waiting in line. It's a familiar scene. We stand and wait to get on the bus, to turn in our essays, to get another serving of mac and cheese. We shift our feet. Stifle yawns. These are the dull moments of our days.

When the waiting is for something exciting, however, dull turns into desperate. Especially if it's for a concert we're dying to see. Especially if the line isn't moving and the concert is almost sold out. Especially if our friends are already inside. *C'mon! What's the holdup? We should be moving!*

Many Christians live with a similar kind of anxiety. Why? They're worried about eternity. They *think* they are saved, *hope* they are saved, but still they doubt, wondering, *Am I* really *saved?*

It's a universal question. Kids who accept Christ ask it. Rebels ask it. It surfaces in the heart of the struggler. It seeps into the thoughts of the dying. When we forget our vow to God, does God forget us? Is our ticket still good, or are heaven's doors closed?

Our behavior gives us reason to wonder. We are strong one day, weak the next. Devoted one hour, delinquent the next. Believing, then unbelieving. Our lives mirror a ride on a roller coaster, highs and lows.

Common wisdom draws a line through the middle of these waves. Perform above this line, and enjoy God's acceptance. But dip below it, and expect a "no vacancy" sign in eternity. In this model, a person is lost and saved multiple times a day, in and out of the kingdom on a regular basis. Salvation becomes a matter of timing. You just hope you die on an upswing. No security, stability, or confidence.

This is not God's plan. He draws the line, yes. But he draws it beneath our ups and downs. Jesus' language couldn't be stronger. "And I give them eternal life, and they shall never lose it or perish throughout the ages. [To all eternity they shall never by any means be destroyed.] And no one is able to snatch them out of My hand" (John 10:28 AMP).

Jesus promised a new life that could not be lost or terminated. "Whoever hears my word and believes him who sent me has eternal life and will not be condemned; he has crossed over from death to life" (John 5:24 NIV). Bridges are burned, and the transfer is accomplished. Ebbs and flows continue, but they never disqualify. Ups and downs may mark our days, but they will never ban us from his kingdom. Jesus bottom-lines our lives with grace.

> Jesus promised a new life that could not be lost or terminated.

Even more, God stakes his claim on us. "By his Spirit he has stamped us with his eternal pledge—a sure beginning of what he is destined to complete" (2 Corinthians 1:22 MSG). You've done something similar: engraved your name on a valued ring, etched your identity on a textbook or iPad. Cowboys brand cattle with the mark of the ranch. Stamping declares ownership.

Through his Spirit, God stamps us. Would-be takers are repelled by the presence of his name. Satan is driven back by the declaration: *Hands off. This child is mine! Eternally, God.*

On-and-off salvation never appears in the Bible. Salvation is not a repeated phenomenon. Scripture contains no example of a person who was saved, then lost, then resaved, then lost again.

Where there is no assurance of salvation, there is no peace. No peace means no joy. No joy results in fear-based lives. Is this the life God creates? No. Grace creates a confident soul who declares, "I couldn't be more sure of my ground—the One I've trusted in can take care of what he's trusted me to do right to the end" (2 Timothy 1:12 MSG).

> Grace is the gift of feeling sure that our future, even our dying, is going to turn out more splendidly than we dare imagine.
>
> —Lewis Smedes

YOUR STORY:

On a scale of 1 to 10, with 10 being "absolutely certain," how confident are you of going to heaven to be with God?

....

What do you base your answer on?

....

Of all we don't know in life, we know this: we hold a ticket. Trust God's hold on you more than your hold on God. His faithfulness does not depend on yours. His performance is not predicated on yours. His love is not contingent on your own. Your candle may flicker, but it will not expire.

> God's faithfulness does not depend on yours.

Do you find such a promise hard to believe? The disciples did.

On the night before his death, Jesus made this announcement: "Tonight you will all fall away because of me. This is because it is written, *I will hit the shepherd, and the sheep of the flock will go off in all directions.* But after I'm raised up, I'll go before you to Galilee" (Matthew 26:31–32 CEB).

By this point the disciples had known Jesus for three years. They'd spent a thousand nights with him. They knew his stride, accent, and sense of humor. They'd smelled his breath, heard him snore, and watched him pick his teeth after dinner. They'd witnessed miracles we know about and countless more we don't. They unwrapped burial clothing from a was-dead Lazarus. They watched mud fall from the eyes of a was-blind man. For three years these handpicked recruits enjoyed front-row, center-court seats to heaven's greatest display. And how would they respond?

"All of you will fall away," Jesus told them. Turn away. Run away. Their promises would melt like wax on a summer sidewalk. Jesus' promise, however, would stay firm. "But after I'm raised up, I will go before you to Galilee" (v. 32). Translation? Your fall will be great, but my grace will be greater. Stumble, I will catch you. Scatter, I will gather you. Turn from me, I will turn toward you. You'll find me waiting for you in Galilee.

The promise was lost on Peter. "Even if all are made to stumble because of You, I will never be made to stumble" (v. 33).

Not one of Peter's finer moments. "Even if all . . ." Arrogant. "I will never be made to stumble." Self-sufficient. Peter's trust was in Peter's strength. Yet Peter's strength would peter out. Jesus knew it. "Simon, I've prayed for you in particular that you not give in or give out. When you have come through the time of testing, turn to your companions and give them a fresh start" (Luke 22:31–32 MSG).

Satan would attack and test Peter. But Satan would never claim Peter. Why? Because Peter was strong? No, because Jesus was. "I've prayed for you." Jesus' prayers for one of his own leave Satan hamstrung. That person may stumble for a while but will not fall away completely.

Jesus prays for you as well. "Holy Father, keep them and care for them—all those you have given me—so that they will be united just as we are. . . . I am praying not only for these disciples but also for all who will ever believe in me because of their testimony" (John 17:11, 20 NLT). Our faith will wane, our resolve will waver, but we will not completely fall away.

Will some people take advantage of this assurance? Knowing that God will catch them if they fall, might they fall on purpose? Yes, they might, for a time. But as grace goes deep, as God's love and kindness sink in, they will change. Grace fosters obedience.

> If I could hear Christ praying for me in the next room, I would not fear a million enemies.
>
> —Robert Murray McCheyne

Consider the story of one boy who turned away.

I WASN'T PREPARED FOR A PRODIGAL

by Gigi Graham Tchividjian

Just five years ago I wondered if I would see my beloved son again. Tullian was our prodigal. His father, Stephan, and I had given him all we could. We loved him dearly, but he chose to disregard his teaching and training and turned his back on all that we offered. We had no choice but to ask him to leave—at sixteen.

I'll never forget the day he left home. I stood in the doorway, watching my son walk slowly down the driveway and out into the street. Then, with a heart that felt heavy as lead, I reluctantly turned away.

I forced myself to go through the motions of fixing dinner and doing the evening chores. When I finally crawled into bed, I lay awake, crying and wondering. Where was he? Had he eaten supper? Did he have a place to sleep? Could we have done things differently? *Would he ever come home again?*

I thought back on the months before that day. The ups and downs, the emotions, the harsh words, the frustrations, the disobedience, the dishonesty, the questions, the long nights . . .

sitting and waiting, wondering, worrying, asking, "Why?" Why was our son choosing to rebel? He could have a warm, loving home, physical comfort, an education, a godly heritage. We had wanted him, prayed for him, and had been overjoyed at his arrival. Tullian had been such a fun-loving, happy child. We called him our "sunshine."

I wasn't prepared for a prodigal. Eventually, when I accepted the fact that God loved my son even more than I did, I was able to surrender Tullian to him. But as the years came and went, I still found myself discouraged. My hopes would build, only to come crashing down in bitter disappointment. I was tempted again and again to try to do God's job for him. Then I would cry the words of the old hymn: "Oh, for grace to trust him more!" And in response I would hear a still, small voice deep within my heart saying, "Love and patience . . . love and patience."

I didn't have a problem with the love part. After all, I'm a mother. But I had a lot of trouble with the patience. My mother reminded me that in dealing with an all-knowing, all-loving, all-powerful God, I had to pray not only with persistence, but with patience.

More years passed. Then, totally unexpectedly, Tullian took his girlfriend by the hand one Sunday, and from high in the balcony of our church, they went forward to give their lives to Jesus Christ.

I was overwhelmed with joy—but also a bit skeptical. I didn't want to have my hopes dashed again. I waited and watched. As the weeks turned into months, we saw this young man grow and mature into a sincere, dedicated child of God.

Recently he wrote these words to an older Christian friend:

Things went real raw after I last saw you. My whole life went down the tubes. I really fell far from the Lord. Drugs, alcohol, sex, the whole nine yards. I dropped out of school, got kicked out of my house; things couldn't have gotten much worse.

But I don't want to go on about the bad stuff. I want to tell you about what the Lord has done for me. After leading a very empty, up-and-down lifestyle, I gave the Lord total control of my life. What a change. Things I used to live for don't even matter anymore. Things I used to run away from, I'm hungry for.

Isn't God good? He has been so patient with me. He never gave up on me. For the first time in my life I feel peace and contentment. I don't worry about anything. I am a totally different person.

Yes, our prodigal had returned.[1]

God's patience stirred Tullian's holiness. God's wild, unquenchable grace does the same in us. If you ever catch yourself thinking, *I can do whatever I want because God will forgive me*, then grace is not happening to you. Selfishness, perhaps. Arrogance, for sure. But grace? No. Grace creates a resolve to do good, not permission to do bad.

> The Law tells me how crooked I am; Grace comes along and straightens me out.
>
> —Dwight L. Moody

Let grace comfort you. Look to Christ for your beginning and ending. He will hold you. And he will hold on to the ones you love. Do you have a prodigal brother or sister? Do you long for your mom or dad to return to God? Do you have a friend whose faith has grown cold? God wants them back more than you do. Keep praying, but don't give up.

Barbara Leininger didn't. She and her sister, Regina, were daughters of German immigrants who had settled in colonial Pennsylvania. On a fall day in 1755, the sisters were in the farm cabin with their brother and father when two Indian warriors slammed open the door. Many of the natives in the area were friendly, but this pair was not. Barbara, eleven, and Regina, nine, huddled together as their father stepped forward. His wife and second son had gone to the mill for the day. They were safe, but his two daughters were not.

He offered the Indians food and tobacco. He told the girls to fetch a bucket of water, that the men must be thirsty. As the girls scurried out the door, he spoke to them in German and told them not to come back until the Indians were gone. They raced toward the nearby creek. As they were drawing water from the creek, a gunshot rang out. They hid in the grass and watched as the cabin went up in flames. Their father and brother never came out, but the two warriors did.

They found the girls hiding in the grass and dragged them away. Other braves and captives soon appeared. Barbara realized that she and Regina were just two of many children who had survived a massacre. Days became weeks as the Indians marched the captives westward. Barbara did her best to stay close to Regina and keep up her spirits. She reminded Regina of the song their mother had taught them:

Alone, yet not alone am I
Though in this solitude so drear
I feel my Savior always nigh;
He comes the weary hours to cheer
I am with Him and He with me
I therefore cannot lonely be.[2]

The girls sang to each other as they fell asleep at night. As long as they were together, they believed they could survive. At a certain point, however, the Indians dispersed, separating the sisters. Barbara attempted to hold on to Regina and released her hand only at threat of death.

The two girls were marched in opposite directions. Barbara's journey continued for several weeks, deeper and deeper into the forest. Finally an Indian village appeared. It became clear that she and the other children were to forget the ways of their parents. No English was permitted, only Iroquoian. They farmed fields and tanned hides. They wore buckskins and moccasins. She lost all contact with her family and fellow settlers.

Three years later Barbara escaped. She ran through the woods for eleven days, finally reaching safety at Fort Pitt. She pleaded with the officers to send a rescue party to look for Regina. They explained to her that such a mission would be impossible and made arrangements for her to be reunited with her mother and brother. No one had news of Regina.

Barbara thought daily of her sister, but her hope had no substance until six years later. She had married and had begun raising her own family when she received word that 206 captives had been rescued and taken to Fort Carlisle. Might Regina be one of them?

Barbara and her mother set off to find out. The sight of the refugees stunned them. Most had spent years isolated in villages, separated from any settlers. They were emaciated and confused. They were so pale they blended in with the snow.

Barbara and her mother walked up and down the line, calling Regina's name, searching faces and speaking German. No one looked or spoke back. The mother and daughter turned away with tears in their eyes and told the colonel that Regina wasn't among the rescued.

The colonel urged them to be sure. He asked about identifying blemishes such as scars or birthmarks. There were none. He asked about heirlooms, a necklace or bracelet. The mother shook her head. Regina had been wearing no jewelry. The colonel had one final idea: was there a childhood memory or song?

The faces of the two women brightened. What about the song they sang each night? Barbara and her mother immediately turned and began to walk slowly up and down the rows. As they walked, they sang, "Alone, yet not alone am I . . ." For a long time no one responded. The faces seemed comforted by the song, but none reacted to it. Then all of a sudden Barbara heard a loud cry. A tall, slender girl rushed out of the crowd toward her mother, embraced her, and began to sing the verse.

Regina had not recognized her mother or sister. She had forgotten how to speak English and German. But she remembered the song that had been placed in her heart as a young girl.[3]

God places a song in the hearts of his children too. A song of hope and life. "He has put a new song in my mouth" (Psalm 40:3). Some Christians sing this song loud and long every single day of their lives. In other cases the song falls silent. Life's hurts and happenings mute the music within. Long seasons pass in which God's song is not sung.

I want to be careful here. Truth is, we do not always know if someone has trusted God's grace. A person may pretend belief but not mean it.[4] It isn't ours to know. But we know this: when we confess our sins and believe in God—not just say the words but truly *believe*—our ticket to eternity is punched. Our seat in heaven is reserved. We are saved for sure. Our task is simply to trust him. His never-ending grace calls us home.

Even when we mess up. Even if we are lost, cut off from his family for years. Eventually we hear his voice, and something within us awakens. And when it does, we begin to sing again.

CONCLUSION

WHEN GRACE HAPPENS

The same work God did through Christ long ago on a cross is the work God does through Christ right now in you.

Ten-year-olds take Christmas gifts very seriously. At least we did in Mrs. Griffin's fourth-grade class. The holiday gift exchange outranked the presidential election, NFL draft, and Fourth of July parade. We knew the procedure well. On the day before Thanksgiving break, Mrs. Griffin wrote each of our names on a piece of paper, dumped the slips of paper into a baseball cap, and shook them up. One by one we stepped up to her desk and drew the name of the person we would give a gift.

Under the Law of Gift Exchange passed down for centuries, we were instructed to keep our target's identity a secret. Name disclosure was not permitted. We told no one for whom we were shopping. But we told everyone what we were wanting. How else would they know? We dropped hints like the Canadian winter drops snow, everywhere and every day. I made certain each classmate knew what I wanted: a Sixfinger.

In 1965, all red-blooded American boys wanted a Sixfinger. We knew the slogan by heart: "Sixfinger, Sixfinger, man alive! How did I ever get along with five?" The Sixfinger was more than a toy. Yes sirree, Bob. It could fire off a cap bomb, message missile, secret bullet, and SOS signal. Why, it even had a hidden ballpoint pen. Who could live without a Sixfinger? I couldn't. And I made certain the other twelve students in Mrs. Griffin's class knew it.

But Carol wasn't listening. Little Carol with the pigtails, freckles, and shiny black shoes. Don't let her sweet appearance fool you. She broke my heart. For on the day of the great gift exchange, I ripped the wrapping paper off my box to find only stationery. You read the word correctly. Stationery! Brown envelopes with folded note cards that bore a picture of a cowboy lassoing a horse. What ten-year-old boy uses stationery?

There is a term for this type of gift: *obligatory*. The required-to-give gift. The "Oops! I almost forgot to get something" gift.

I can envision the scene at Little Carol's house on that fateful morning in 1965. She is eating breakfast. Her mother raises the question of the class Christmas party. "Carol, are you supposed to take any gifts to class?"

Little Carol drops her spoon into her Rice Krispies. "I forgot! I'm supposed to bring a gift for Max."

"For whom?"

"For Max, my handsome classmate who excels in every sport and subject and is utterly polite and humble in every way."

"And you're just now telling me?" Carol's mom asks.

"I forgot. But I know what he wants. He wants a Sixfinger."

"An extra finger?"

"No. A Sixfinger. 'Sixfinger, Sixfinger, man alive! How did I ever get along with five?'"

Carol's mom scoffs at the thought. "Humph. Sixfinger my aunt Edna." She goes to the storage closet and begins rummaging through . . . well, rummage. She finds paisley tube socks her son discarded and a dinosaur-shaped scented candle. She almost selects the box of Bic pens, but then she spies the stationery.

Carol falls to her knees and pleads, "Don't do it, Mom. Don't give him stationery with a little cowboy lassoing a horse. Forty-seven years from now he will describe this moment in the conclusion of a book. Do you really want to be memorialized as the one who gave an obligatory gift?"

"Bah humbug," Carol's mom objects. "Give him the stationery. That kid is destined for prison anyway. He will have plenty of time to write letters there."

And so she gave me the gift. And what did I do with it? The same thing you did with those ridiculous musical socks your aunt sent you. I gave it away at the class Christmas party the next year.

I know we shouldn't complain. But, honestly, when someone hands you Christmas candy from two years ago and says, "This is for you," don't you detect a lack of creativity? But when a person gives a genuine gift, don't you cherish the presence of affection? The home-baked cookies, the tickets to see your favorite obscure band, the personalized poem, the Lucado book. Such gifts convince you that someone

> Grace is precious because he is. Grace changes lives because he does.

planned, prepared, saved, searched. Last-minute decision? No, this gift was just for you.

Have you ever received such a gift? Yes, you have. Sorry to speak on your behalf, but I know the answer as I ask the question. You have been given a perfect personal gift. One just for you. "There has been born *for you* a Savior, who is Christ the Lord" (Luke 2:11 NASB, emphasis mine).

An angel spoke these words. Shepherds heard them first. But what the angel said to them, God says to anyone who will listen. "There has been born *for you* . . ." Jesus is the gift.

He himself is the treasure. Grace is precious because he is. Grace changes lives because he does. Grace secures us because he will. The gift is the Giver: "The grace of God that brings salvation has appeared" (Titus 2:11).

> Grace is power, not just pardon.
>
> —John Piper

To discover grace is to discover God's total devotion to you, his stubborn resolve to give you a cleansing, healing, purging love that lifts the wounded back to their feet. Does he stand high on a hill and bid you climb out of the valley? No. He bungees down and carries you out. Does he build a bridge and command you to cross it? No. He crosses the bridge and shoulders you over.

This is the gift that God gives. A grace that grants us first the power to receive love and then the power to give it. A grace that changes us, shapes us, and leads us to a life that is forever altered. Do you know this grace? Do you trust this grace? If not, you can. All God wants from us is faith. Put your faith in God.

Let him do his work. Let grace outshine your bad grades, critics, and guilty conscience. See yourself for what you are—God's personal remodeling project. Not a world to yourself but a work in his hands. No longer defined by failures but refined by them. Trusting less in what you do and more in what Christ did. Not without grace but overflowing with it. Convinced down deep in the center of your soul that God is just getting started in your life.

And grow in God's grace. More action than idea. More now than then. Grace didn't just happen; it happens. Grace happens here.

> See yourself for what you are—God's personal remodeling project.

The same work God did through Christ long ago on a cross is the work God does through Christ right now in you.

NOTES

Chapter 1: The Grace Adventure
1. My late friend Tim Hansel said something similar in his book *You Gotta Keep Dancin'* (Elgin, IL: David C. Cook Publishing Co., 1985), 107.
2. Shannon Ethridge, "Why Didn't He Hate Me?" *Christianity Today*, January 1, 2008, http://www.christianitytoday.com/iyf /truelifestories/ithappenedtome/10.44.html.

Chapter 2: No More Critics
1. Adapted from Josh Phillips as told to Ann Swindell, "If Anybody Knew the Real Me," *Christianity Today*, January 1, 2008, http://www .christianitytoday.com/iyf/truelifestories/ithappenedtome/20.40.html.
2. Jim Reimann, *Victor Hugo's Les Misérables* (Nashville, TN: Word Publishing, 2001), 16.
3. Ibid., 29–31.

Chapter 3: The Best Trade You'll Ever Make
1. Adapted from "Teen Accused of Bomb Threat Spends 12 Days in Juvenile Detention After Daylight-Saving Time Snafu," *Fox News*, April 5, 2007, http://www.foxnews.com/story/0,2933,264273,00.html and from Rich Cholodofsky, "Hempfield Bomb Threat Lawsuit Settled," *Tribune-Review*, August 28, 2008, http://www.pittsburghlive.com/x /pittsburghtrib/news/westmoreland/s_585274.html#.
2 Steve Farrar, *Standing Tall* (Sisters, OR: Multnomah, 1994, 2001), 56–59.
3. Dr. James and Shirley Dobson, *Night Light for Parents* (Sisters, OR: Multnomah, 2002), 130. Used by permission of James Dobson.

Chapter 4: Grace Is All We Need
1. John Newton, "Amazing Grace," HymnSite.com, http://www.hymnsite .com/lyrics/umh378.sht.
2. Adapted from *Fierce Beauty: Choosing to Stand for What Matters Most*, copyright © 2011 by Kim Meeder. Used by permission of WaterBrook Multnomah, an imprint of the Crown Publishing Group, a division of Random House, Inc.

Chapter 5: Rich with Grace

1. Michael Quintanilla, "Angel Gives Dying Father Wedding Moment," *San Antonio Express-News*, December 15, 2010. Used by permission of Chrysalis Autry.
2. Eugene Peterson, *Traveling Light: Modern Meditations on St. Paul's Letter of Freedom* (Colorado Springs, CO: Helmers and Howard, 1988), 91.
3. Adapted from Jacob Andrew Shepherd, "The Christmas I Got Rich," in *Stories for a Teen's Heart, Book 3* (Sisters, OR: Multnomah, 2002), 15–17. Used by permission of Jacob Shepherd.

Chapter 6: Wet Feet

1. David Jeremiah, *Captured by Grace: No One Is Beyond the Reach of a Loving God* (Nashville, TN: Thomas Nelson, 2006), 9–10.
2. Dave Stone, "Ten Years Later: Love Prevails" (sermon, Southeast Christian Church, Louisville, KY, September 11, 2011), http://www .southeastchristian.org/default.aspx?page=3476&project=107253.
3. Adapted from Katherine Bond, "Music Lessons," in *Stories for the Extreme Teen's Heart*, comp. Alice Gray (Sisters, OR: Multnomah, 2000), 42–46. Used by permission of Katherine Grace Bond, the author of the YA novel *The Summer of No Regrets* (Sourcebooks) and children's book *The Legend of the Valentine* (Zondervan), a story of the Civil Rights Movement.
4. Jeremiah, *Captured by Grace*, 11.
5. Robin Finn, "Pushing Past the Trauma to Forgiveness," *New York Times*, October 28, 2005, http://www.nytimes.com/2005/10/28 /nyregion/28lives.html.
6. Jonathan Lemire, "Victoria Ruvolo, Who Was Hit by Turkey Nearly 6 Years Ago, Forgives Teens for Terrible Prank," *New York Daily News*, November 7, 2010, http://articles.nydailynews.com/2010-11-07 /local/27080547_1_victoria-ruvolo-ryan-cushing-forgives.
7. Ibid.

Chapter 7: Fessing Up

1. Adapted from Shaun Groves, "Addicted to Porn," *Christianity Today*, January 1, 2007, http://www.christianitytoday.com/iyf/hottopics /sexabstinence/15.50.html.Used by permission of Shaun Groves.
2. "Doctors Remove Knife from Man's Head After 4 Years," AOL News, February 18, 2011, http://www.aolnews.com/2011/02/18/doctors-remove-knife-from-li-fuyans-head-after-4-years.

Chapter 8: Better Than Perfect

1. Adapted from Carla Barnhill, "If Only I Could Be Perfect," *Christianity Today*, http://www.christianitytoday.com/iyf/hottopics /selfesteem/8c6040.html. This article first published in *Campus Life*. Used by permission. Copyright Christianity Today International.
2. From Katherine Leal Unmuth and Joe Simnacher, "Coppell Teen Who Died in Ski Accident Remembered for Her Vitality," *Dallas Morning News*, March 17, 2010, http://www.dallasnews.com/news /community-news/coppell/headlines/20100316-Coppell-teen-who-died-in-ski-7917.ece.

Chapter 9: You Belong

1. Michael T. Powers, "A Father's Love," in *Chicken Soup for the Christian Teenage Soul* (Deerfield Beach, FL: Health Communications, 2003), 73–75.
2. Adapted from LaDonna Gatlin, "Outstretched Arms," from *Chicken Soup for the Soul: Christian Teen Talk* by Jack Canfield, Mark Victor Hansen & Amy Newmark. Copyright 2008 by Chicken Soup for the Soul Publishing, LLC. Published by Chicken Soup for the Soul Publishing, LLC. Chicken Soup for the Soul is a registered trademark of Chicken Soup for the Soul Publishing, LLC. Reprinted by permission. All rights reserved.
3. Lee Nailling, "Orphan Train," in *Guideposts*, March 1991.

Chapter 10: Saved for Sure

1. From *Currents of the Heart: Glimpses of God in the Stream of Life* by Gigi Graham Tchividjian, copyright © 1996 by Gigi Graham Tchividjian. Used by permission of WaterBrook Multnomah, an imprint of the Crown Publishing Group, a division of Random House, Inc.
2. Tracy Leininger Craven, *Alone, Yet Not Alone* (San Antonio, TX: His Seasons, 2001), 19.
3. Ibid., 29–31, 42, 153–54, 176, 190–97.
4. Judas is an example of one who seemed to have been saved but in truth was not. For three years he followed Christ. While the others were becoming apostles, he was becoming a tool of Satan. When Jesus said, "You are clean, though not every one of you" (John 13:10 NIV), he was referring to Judas, who possessed a fake faith. Persistent sin can betray nonbelief.